THE ZOTERO SOLUTION

THE ZOTERO SOLUTION

KNOWLEDGE MANAGEMENT
for the
SCHOLARLY RESEARCHER

by

Donna Cox Baker

Golden Channel Publishing
TUSCALOOSA, ALABAMA

Limited portions of this text have appeared in blog postings by Donna Cox Baker on the Golden Egg Genealogist website at geg-bound.com. Substantial sections were published in *Zotero for Genealogy: Harnessing the Power of Your Research*.

ISBN 978-0-9996899-3-6

Library of Congress Control Number: 2019957961

Golden Channel Publishing
6552 Ash Hill Drive
Tuscaloosa, Alabama 35405

Visit goldenchannelpublishing.com and join us on Facebook at https://www.facebook.com/The-Zotero-Solution-Knowledge-Management-for-the-Scholarly-Researcher-111777490324836/. Sign up for news, tips, and product update information at https://tinyurl.com/GetGCPMail.

For my alma maters

TABLE OF CONTENTS

ACKNOWLEDGMENTS

I do not recall the first person who told me I should consider the Zotero software. Nor the second or third. I am grateful to all who sounded the call until I eventually looked beneath the hood and saw the power it offered.

I am grateful to the Corporation for Digital Scholarship for supporting this gem. And I thank George Mason University, the Andrew W. Mellon Foundation, the Institute of Museum and Library Services, the Alfred P. Sloan Foundation, and every other organization or individual who has funded this work and kept Zotero free. I thank Zotero forum superheroes Dan Stillman and Adam Smith, often the "first responders" to essential forum questions over the years.

I thank the readers of *Zotero for Genealogy: Harnessing the Power of Your Research*, my first book on Zotero. Their emails and forum posts continue to bring me new insights and greater clarity on what Zotero can do. Their creative uses for this product continue to expand my awareness and effectiveness in its use.

As I turn my attention back to my days in graduate school, where my Zotero awareness began, I feel gratitude to all the institutions that had a role in teaching me research and writing, from that first eleventh-grade "term paper." I dedicate this to all my alma maters: Shades Valley High School, the University of Montevallo, Auburn University, the University of Alabama at Birmingham, and the University of Alabama.

PREFACE

Zotero revolutionized graduate school for me. This reference management and notetaking tool minimized the pain and hassle of gathering research, organizing it, analyzing it, and formatting it for research papers, my dissertation, and publications. It allowed me to put my energy and time into learning and writing, rather than into the mechanics of citations and recordkeeping.

After graduate school for a doctorate in history, I turned my passion and attention back to my first love: genealogy. Zotero has only proven more useful with every article I clip, document I find, or publication I prepare.

While in the corporate world, before graduate school, I was drawn to the burgeoning field of knowledge management and became its proponent to my employer—a Fortune 500 computer company. Knowledge management used technology to gather and capture for reuse the shared knowledge of our personnel. I now use the term for the management of the knowledge I harness by research.

This product is excellent for academic research management. Here is just a brief sampling of what Zotero offers the student, professor, or independent researcher:

- Eliminates paper and physical filing, replacing every notecard, file cabinet, notebook, binder, box, and paper stack that could weigh you down.

- Eliminates thousands of keystrokes as Zotero gathers reference records for citations from online resources with the click of a button.
- Creates your citations and bibliographies for you in Microsoft Word, LibreDocs, OpenOffice, or Google Docs with dynamic connections to your Zotero data.
- Accesses your citations and notes virtually anywhere you have Wi-Fi and a computing device.
- Stores or creates a gateway to all the digital articles, images, spreadsheets, documents, audio and video files and other materials you collect in your research.
- Extracts the comments you have made and the passages you have highlighted in a text-editable PDF, drawing them into Zotero without retyping.
- Finds anything you have stored, with lightning-fast smart searching—even things you stored years ago and remember only vaguely if at all.
- Allows you to plan your research and keep up with what you have done and what you intend to do.
- Builds a smart research to-do list that eliminates repetitive data entry and is there whenever you need it.
- Allows a group of scholars to collaborate on research.
- Facilitates the reuse of research for multiple projects without duplicating effort or records.

Zotero is a workhorse, a powerhouse, a just plain fantastic knowledge management tool. And here's the best part—the most unbelievable part:

It's FREE.*

You have nothing to lose in giving this a try. You are about to have control over your research at last.

Here is another consideration. Your university may offer you free access to expensive software while you are a student or faculty member. Before you accept that offer, think about

---

* Zotero is worth a mint at no charge. Once you discover its value, I encourage you to consider contributing to the Corporation for Digital Scholarship. You may also opt to use Zotero as your storage cloud for attachments, in which case, there is a very reasonable charge. Storage funding supports the Zotero development team.

this: The articles, lectures, and books you write—and the research that supports it—may be serving you for the rest of your career. When you graduate or change employers, will you find yourself now having to buy the expensive software in order to read your old records? I found that Zotero gave me everything the expensive software offered and more. And now, I can still look at sources I remember from long-ago papers, drawing that information into new work I am doing. Zotero is always accessible and has for decades now been free.

No matter where I go, it can go with me. Read on to empower your research.

1: INTRODUCTION

I almost let Zotero pass me by, for the most superficial of reasons. In graduate school, I heard scholars say they were using it for their research. I gave it a quick look a couple of times, but I perceived two strikes against it.

First, Zotero is plain-looking. I have been persuaded to buy relatively worthless books (once a nine-volume set) because I loved the covers, I confess. But surely something this plain showed a lack of care about marketing the product, I thought. So why should I trust it?

Second, Zotero is free. I have never trusted free when it comes to software. There always comes the "catch"—that moment when you realize what *free* has cost you. Perhaps you do

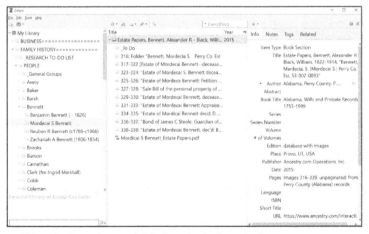

Plain-looking, free, and fabulous, it challenged all my stereotypes.

1

work of value in the new software, then discover you must purchase the premium version to save your work or print it.

I tried the most expensive research management tool on the market, wanting the edge in graduate school. Five hundred dollars, and it kept crashing and corrupting my data. I created my own Access database, which served for a while, but I wasted huge amounts of time trying to create my own "features."

By a stroke of great luck one day, I heard a scholar describe a feature in Zotero that sounded impossible: the Zotero Connector, which I will describe in Chapter 8. I had to try it, and as a free product, I had nothing to lose. For the first time, I gave Zotero a serious look, and that is the day research changed for me. This was everything I had tried to get out of other products and even some things I never imagined I could have. Now, after a decade with Zotero, it continues to serve my work beautifully.

I soon realized why the developers of Zotero have not invested in the superficial things like good looks. They are not trying to sell it. It is a contribution to the world of research, originally developed by a global community through the Roy Rosenzweig Center for History and New Media at Virginia's George Mason University. This product, used worldwide by scholars in many fields, has the vetting and support of the Corporation for Digital Scholarship. It is far less likely to suffer the fate of so many products—obsolescence in a rapidly changing computer environment or being bought up, subsumed, and destroyed by a bigger fish.

Without the need to lure buyers with fancy and memory-intensive pretty interfaces, Zotero's creators have put their focus on what matters most to us: getting the job done well.

WHAT IS ZOTERO?

Zotero's makers describe it in this simple and understated way:

> *Zotero [zoh-TAIR-oh] is a free, easy-to-use tool to help you collect, organize, cite, and share your research sources.*

Stacks and boxes, file cabinets and bulging bookshelves, once stood as the physical evidence of a scholar at work. A new generation can have decades of work with them at all times, and they can quickly find what they stored.

As the years pass, I keep finding more uses for Zotero. I store ideas for future projects there, career and personal. I journal there. I capture home do-it-yourself advice from the Internet. It has become my engine for knowledge management. In a world where "know-how" grows exponentially, we must have a place to keep the knowledge before the next piece of information forces it to the deep recesses of memory. And we need a tool powerful enough to draw it up again, long after all memory of a golden piece of information has vanished.

Zotero offers both structure and flexibility in your management of knowledge. It captures the information you need to gather, compile, and analyze research data; cite sources; work collaboratively with others; research anywhere; and turn ideas and information scraps into well-thought-out papers, articles, and books. It blends the structure of controlled databases—encouraging careful citation development—with much of the flexibility you find in notetaking software like Evernote and OneNote.

It presents structured forms for the established bibliographic style standards and variants for most academic fields. More than 9,500 style variations were available to Zotero users as of this book's publication. You can draw up different sets of citation fields, depending upon the type of source you are citing. This allows a smart focus on what matters as you are working, eliminating wasted time on perfecting footnotes.

With Zotero, you can create voluminous notes in plain or formatted text, fully searchable and organized to suit your filing preferences. You can attach or link to material in numerous forms—documents of various types, spreadsheets, images, videos, audio files, and others.

One of the main powers of Zotero lies in the fact that its makers offer it "open source." In other words, programmers can build on to it, offering extra features. And they have. Wonderful features. Also, usually free.

Placing function over aesthetic form, Zotero offers the environment that can give you real management of the knowledge you are mastering and/or creating. You can truly go paperless, your computer replacing the mountain of paper or the hard drive filled with hard-to-find files you might have collected, doing research the old way. This is a new way, a better way, a smarter way.

How does Zotero serve scholars?

You might be wondering what Zotero gives you that you do not already have in Google Docs or Evernote or your spiral-bound notebook or index cards, or whatever tool you have tended to use to take notes. Zotero serves scholars in many ways, from storage and retrieval of data to work planning and collaboration. We will examine many of its functions in-depth in later chapters, but the descriptions below will give you a sense of why this is a tool worth cultivating.

Your research storage and retrieval system

Zotero can replace the file cabinets, binders, boxes, folders, and stacks of unfiled photocopies that the new generations of scholars dread and avoid. It becomes the "brain" connecting you to the mass of documents, photos, spreadsheets, digital recordings, and maps you are collecting.

It creates a low-stress, high-yield organizational structure. You do not have to worry so much about putting just the right label on a file folder or document—afraid you will never find it again. Zotero sports such a great search mechanism that you can find things that would have been lost to you forever in other systems.

Let's say you have a vague recollection that you once found a magazine article from the late 1800s that mentioned the easy access to opium at a neighborhood apothecary. You are studying opiates, so nearly every document you have includes a variation of the word opium. You do not remember where you saw it or how you would have filed it, but it is critical to a point you want to make in an essay you are writing.

Your old paper filing system would not make this easy to find. Even if you are using an online notetaking system like OneNote, you could search a very long time. But in Zotero, you can retrieve magazine articles, exclusively—articles you have collected from the late 1800s that mention the word "apothecary" or "druggist." You can tell it to eliminate any that fail to mention "opium" or "opiate." And you watch the search results reduce to a manageable few. It works with our faulty memory to make our research findable again.

Even better, you can store more and more without any change in the bulk and weight of your research. Your six-pound laptop will still be six pounds as your research entries multiply. You will be amazed at how fast your searches are, even as your records begin to number in the thousands.

Zotero also eliminates an information storage problem that plagues some fields of study. Let's say you are doing research on a group of people and have a file on each one. Your research might uncover a document that mentions 20 of your subjects on the same page. With traditional filing, you might feel compelled to make 20 copies of the source, filing a copy in each folder for 20 people. If you discover you left a vital piece of citation information out of the original, you must correct it in 20 places.

With Zotero, on the other hand, you can create just one record and any desirable notes. Then you drag it into an online folder for every person—or every place or every topic—it references. While it then appears everywhere, it only exists once. If you change the record once, you have changed it everywhere.

Your citation system

While notetaking software like OneNote and Evernote can be very nice for collecting fragments of information, the absence of a systematic source citation structure has drawbacks. Zotero knows what information you are supposed to gather from sources to meet the *Chicago Manual of Style* (*CMOS*), *Modern Language Association* (MLA), or *American Psychological Association* (APA) style standards or another of the thousands of style standards it offers. If you tell it you are gathering information from a newspaper, it presents you with the citation data fields your chosen style requires to cite a newspaper.

You can turn your Zotero citations into proper footnotes, endnotes, or bibliographical records in papers, articles, or books you write. You can copy and paste or drag and drop citation information easily. It essentially puts a dialog box into your Microsoft Word (or Google Docs, OpenOffice, or LibreOffice) environment that lets you grab data out of Zotero with a few keystrokes, creating the citations.

Your to-do list

Zotero has never marketed itself as to-do software. I happened upon its brilliance for organizing research tasks by accident. I will cover it in more detail in Chapter 13, but the combination of a Zotero add-on that lets you capture bibliographic citations

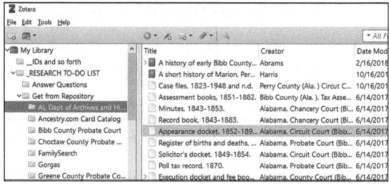

Zotero becomes a robust to-do list for your research trips, preparing you to capture research notes, and creating your post-research follow-up tickler as you go.

in a single click and Zotero's organizational "collection" structure gives you a real power in planning research trips or tasks.

When a source comes to your attention—something you want to follow up on later—you can create the tickler for yourself and have a robust roadmap to the research you want to do in any given place. The most tedious part of research—citation writing—has already been done for you. You simply need to add notes. The information you have gathered then becomes your tickler file for the work needed to follow up after a research trip, processing the information you found.

Your collaboration tool with other researchers

Scholars often work in teams, and Zotero facilitates this. It allows you to share the work you are doing, so everyone in your team can find what has been done. You can create an environment in which multiple people are adding to and borrowing from the same set of research notes.

Your portable wonder

Scholars need portability of their research for so many reasons. Your research may take you anywhere in the world (or anywhere in town or to the park). In packing, you never know what tidbit of information you will need from your files to make sense of the next piece of information you gather. You never know when an hour will open up on an unrelated trip, allowing you to do unplanned work in an archive. And if your career takes you to a new place, you will want to take your research with you, even if your next employer does not offer the same software your current one does.

HOW SHOULD I USE THIS BOOK?

Many, maybe even most, of you will learn best by reading through this book front to back. It will bring you knowledge in the order you need it. You will learn about things in one chapter that serve you in the next. You might even prefer to read it completely before applying any of it.

Let me confess up front, though, that I have never had the patience to learn so systematically. I want to install the software and start playing with it. I usually come to a software book with a specific question in my mind—something I want the software to do. And until I answer that question, nothing else will stick in my nonlinear mind. That will work here, too. Use the Table of Contents or the Index to look for answers to your questions.

For my nonlinear friends, our experimental learning can be powerful in leading us to places the book does not go. But there is also the risk that we will miss something useful in bouncing through the text. So, I encourage you to scan the Table of Contents a few times throughout your self-education, in case there are uses for Zotero that never occurred to you.

In the next chapter, I will show you how to download some sample citations and notes that will be of use as we go through the material in the book. I will also have you creating and changing some of the material in exercises, as we go through. So, again, to the nonlinear ones who want to bounce through, rather than reading front to back, know that you may not be looking at the examples, as intended. At least, download the samples, as instructed.

In the interest of making this book clear and concise, I will be writing about Zotero as I see it, rather than translating the differences for those on other platforms. Know this: Zotero's desktop software works for Windows, macOS, and Linux operating systems. I am on Windows 10, Zotero 5, and I use Microsoft Office 365 in creating my attachments and demonstrating certain add-ons. You might have to make minor adaptations to instructions if you are a Mac or Linux user or have a different version of Windows or office software. Your workspace might look slightly different. But generally, the instructions should guide you reasonably well through the essential steps. If you are using a smartphone or tablet, rather than a desktop, you will work directly in Zotero.org's online product. See Chapter 14 for more information

I have divided the book into three parts, to guide us through the process:

Part I   Introduces the basic functions of Zotero, applicable to anyone using the software.

Part II   Describes several add-on features, external tools that expand Zotero's power in invaluable ways.

Part III   Applies Zotero to the complexities of scholarly research projects.

Enough, then, about what we are going to do. Let's start *doing* Zotero.

PART I:

ZOTERO GENERAL OVERVIEW

Part I describes the installation, setup, and essential functions of Zotero. It will guide you to a set of materials online that you can download and use to illuminate the examples and exercises in the text.

2: GETTING STARTED WITH ZOTERO

This chapter will take you through the basics of installing and setting up Zotero, finding your way around its environment, syncing your work, and getting online help.

INSTALLING ZOTERO

Zotero offers a simple and straightforward installation, which will work much like other standard installations on your computer.

Go to the Zotero home site at zotero.org. Click the Download button to find your software download options on the left

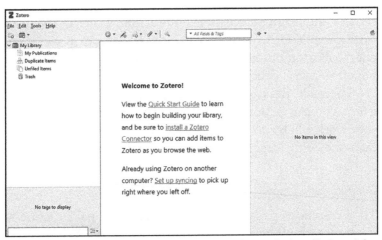

Zotero launches with a welcome screen that facilitates the installation of the Zotero Connector and the setup of your syncing.

13

side of the window. For Windows users, click Download. Mac and Linux users may download Zotero by clicking on the appropriate link just below the Windows option.

Upon launching Zotero, you will see the main workspace and a welcome screen that remain accessible only until you add your first citation. These links guide you to or through several things of value—all of which can be returned to later by different methods. We will do things in a different order than suggested on the welcome screen.

The "Quick Start Guide" gives brief definitions of various Zotero components and might be a good refresher for you later. We will be covering everything in more detail, as we go through this book. While the link is available here, you might want to bookmark the page for later use. Once the welcome screen disappears, you can find it at

https://www.zotero.org/support/quick_start_guide

The other two links will be discussed as we go. The Zotero Connector is the subject of Chapter 8, and we will set up your syncing later in this chapter.

THE ZOTERO WORKSPACE

Zotero's workspace is designed very simply, with most of its content and features accessible on or within a click of the main workspace. Your workspace will be nearly empty as we begin, but the illustrations here will show you what it looks like as you populate it with data.

The main desktop window includes four panes, three of which you can remove from sight when it is helpful. Most of your work will be done in these panes, which are interactive— each one being affected by choices made in the others.

Collections

The Collections pane displays your organizational structure— in essence, the folders to hold your information. You can create multiple layers of subfolders to control your collections further, going far deeper in nested folders than most of us would ever need for our filing.

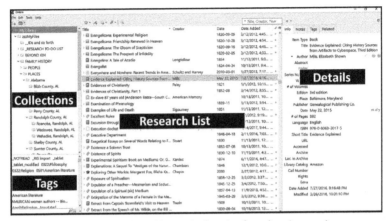

The bulk of your work in Zotero is done in these four interactive panes, displayed here in the default Standard View.

Research List

We will refer to the center pane as your Research List pane. The research list displayed at any given time depends on what you have selected in the Collections pane. At the top of Collections, you will see *My Library*. When you click on it, the Research List pane displays a master list of every research item you have documented. This allows you to search across all your records simultaneously or to sort them by various criteria.

Details

The right-most pane has four tabs to allow the gathering of citation information and research notes, the assignment of "tags" or subject headings, and the ability to relate one citation or note to another. When you select a source reference record in your research list, this pane will show the citation information. If you select a note you have created, the note will display in this pane.

Tags

The Tags pane at the bottom left allows you to filter your view to include only those Zotero items assigned a specific tag—in essence, a subject heading.

CHOOSING YOUR PREFERENCES

We will be talking about various preference settings as we get into deeper discussions of features, but let's take a quick glance at the available settings. From the menu, choose **Edit—Preferences**. The toolbar across the top allows you to set preferences in six different categories.

The Preferences toolbar

General Establishes the preferred workspace view and preferences for the way Zotero will handle materials imported, saved, attached, or copied, among other functions.

Sync Manages the syncing of your data to Zotero's available cloud storage, including choices about the handling of attachments.

Search Sets options affecting search speed and the indexing of the contents of embedded PDFs. Primarily for advanced users.

Export Determines nature and format of information to be exported or copied out of Zotero to other environments. Primarily for advanced users.

Cite Selects style standards, inclusion of URLs in citations, modification of styles, and installation of word processing add-ons.

Advanced

> Sets language options, sets the paths to file storage on the user's personal hard drive, creates keyboard shortcuts, and sets options for advanced users.

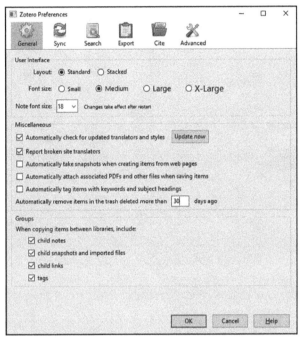

The Preferences view allows you to tailor Zotero for your ideal purposes—everything from its look and feel to its connection to exterior programs and files.

SETTING UP YOUR FREE ZOTERO ACCOUNT

Before we get to the business of adding information to Zotero, let's address the vital need to protect your information. Zotero creates a copy of your data, if you have set it up with automatic syncing, and makes it available for remote access through its cloud sync function.

NOTE: This step is required, if you plan to connect to the sample data created for the exercises.

Zotero offers you 300 MB of free storage for syncing your research. You can make that storage last a very long time by linking rather than embedding attachments (see Chapter 5). But do not worry if you have masses of resource-intensive data you want to embed. Zotero offers unlimited data storage for a reasonable price.

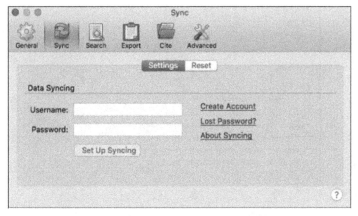

Set up a Zotero account to sync your data.

To sync your data for the first time, you need to establish an account with Zotero.

Step 1   On the menu, choose **Edit—Preferences**.

Step 2   Click the **Sync** button on the toolbar.

Step 3   Click **Create Account** and follow Zotero's instructions to establish your account.

Step 4   Return to the Data Syncing window, enter the Username and Password set up in Step 3, and click **Set Up Syncing**.

Step 5   Accept the defaults on Zotero's Sync panel for the moment. As we look at the choices related to attachments later, you might want to alter these values.

RETRIEVING SAMPLE DATA

As we go through the various instructions and exercises in the chapters ahead, you will benefit from having a set of practice data, which you can get from the Zotero website. You can do this by joining my online Zotero group, which will open the dataset on your own computer. Follow these instructions:

Step 1 Close your desktop Zotero software.

Step 2 Go to https://www.zotero.org/groups/ in your internet browser.

Step 3 If you are not already logged in, click **Log In** in the top-right corner, and enter your username and password.

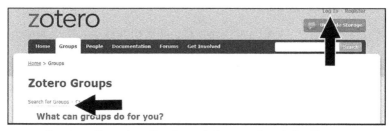

Log in to Zotero's online site and choose to Search for Groups.

Step 4 Click **Search for Groups**, just below the page title.

Step 5 In the search box, type "Baker's Z Solution" and click **Search Groups**.

Step 6 In the search results, click on the title **Baker's Z Solution**.

Step 7 On the right-hand side of the screen, click the **Join** button to obtain access.

Step 8 Close Zotero.org and reopen your desktop software.

Step 9 In the Collections pane, look toward the bottom for *Group Libraries*. (If it is not there, make sure you have followed the instructions above to set up your syncing.)

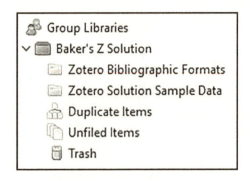

Beneath *Group Libraries*, you should now see a gold folder called *Baker's Z Solution*. Nested under this, you should see two yellow folders titled *Zotero Bibliographic Formats* and *Zotero Solution Sample Data*. (If you do not see them, click on the arrow to the left of the gold folder to expand the contents.)

Drag and drop the subfolders on *My Library*, which is at the top of the Collections pane. The folders will now be copied to the new location—appearing in both places. We will work in the copies in *My Library* for our exercises.

ZOTERO'S DATA STORAGE

To determine where Zotero is storing your data by default, go to Edit—Preferences—Advanced and click the **Files and Folders** tab. The Data Directory Location will show you where your Zotero files are installed, and where data will be stored, unless you opt for another place. If you choose to embed attachments into your Zotero database (see Chapter 5), your attachments will be stored in subfolders of the Storage folder in your data directory.

IMPORTANT NOTE: Zotero stores a single copy of your last synced data. It does not keep multiple copies of older versions. Therefore you should back up your Zotero data regularly, keeping older copies.

ZOTERO SECURITY

Zotero is designed as an open-source product. It does not secure your data. Your research will be as secure as your computer is. If you share your computer with others, your Zotero content is available. Therefore, do not use Zotero as a password keeper.

You may keep multiple Zotero libraries, if it is helpful. If you want to have work-related Zotero information on your work computer and your home computer but want to keep a personal version of Zotero only on your home computer, you may do that with separate profiles. These will be described in Chapter 11.

GETTING HELP

Zotero offers several avenues to assistance, when you have questions. While Zotero has no support hotline, its documentation, troubleshooting guidelines, and forums have assisted me very well for everything I have ever needed. You also have a mechanism to report errors to the programming staff. All these help features can be accessed through the Help menu.

Documentation

Zotero covers the essentials in its online documentation. Many features are not formally documented, however. They are mentioned as part of forum discussions or not at all. While this book does not claim or attempt to cover every detail of setting up and using the software, it will describe many of the hidden tools.

Troubleshooting information

Zotero's online troubleshooting page guides you through the steps you need to follow before escalating a perceived problem to Zotero's staff. It will ensure you are on the most up-to-date version of the software. It will offer you a report of all known issues with the software. And it offers Frequently Asked Questions to cover the typical issues.

Forums

I have found the forums to be remarkably helpful in getting resolutions to issues. Zotero staff, experts on the various styles, and power users typically monitor the forums and usually respond very quickly. I do not recall ever posting a question that was not speedily and effectively answered. You will need your Zotero login to post a message to the board.

Report errors

If the Zotero software generates an error, you can choose the Report Errors option from the Help menu, follow the prompts, and send the error to Zotero for investigation.

Updating your Zotero software

Zotero will routinely check for the availability of a newer version of the software. Or you may force it to check by clicking "Check for Updates" on the Help menu.

SUMMARY

By now, you should have Zotero installed and a Zotero account set up online. You should have sample data in your workspace for use in the exercises we will do throughout the book. We are ready to get to the details of entering basic research.

3: Documenting Your Research

Zotero offers flexibility and shortcuts in citing research and gathering notes. We will start with the basics here, adding more layers of usefulness as we get into the discussions of add-ons and specific applications for Zotero in later chapters.

Choosing your citation style

Zotero will guide you in recording the essential source reference information for your research. It will output a formatted citation, based on the citation style you choose. For students, your instructor will likely assign a style you must use. For scholars anticipating publication, your publisher will have style guidelines. Most scholarly fields have their own preferred citation style standard. In the absence of other mandates, you will want to use that standard.

Zotero supports thousands of different citation styles, and the number keeps growing to support the needs of various scholarly fields, subspecialty variations, and publishing environments. The humanities fields tend to favor the *Chicago Manual of Style* (*CMOS*), and it is usually preferred by most university presses. It is the standard in my field of history, also, so I will use it in this guide.

You may shift from one style to another, though some data, optimized for one style, might not translate perfectly to another. One style might require that you include the name of the country, as you cite a publisher's location, and another wants only the city and state, for U.S. cities. If your field of study has competing standards, become familiar with the differences and make certain you err on the side of gathering too much information, rather than too little. You will then be prepared, should a publisher require you to shift to an alternate style.

To set your default style, select **Edit—Preferences** and choose **Cite** from the toolbar. For our examples here, I am selecting

The Chicago Manual of Style 17th edition (full note)[*]

Select your preferred style and check the box to **Include URLs of paper articles in references**. (You may later choose to deselect this if you do not want the lengthy URL addresses in your citations.) Then, click **OK** to return to the main window.

VIEWING THE RESEARCH LIST

Let's look now at items in your Research List, so you can get familiar with how Zotero structures and displays them. In the Collections pane to the left, under *My Library*, click on the folder called *Zotero Solution Sample Data*. A set of records will appear in the Research List pane.

You will notice to the left of each source citation appearing in your Research List one of a varied set of icons representing the type of source. Next to books, you will see the image of a book, a document icon beside a document, a graduation cap beside a thesis, and so on.

One of the great powers of Zotero lies in its ability to guide you to the information you might need to gather for all the different types of citations. It bases its guidance on the type of item you choose—book, newspaper, website, and so forth.

---

[*] *CMOS* is in its 17th edition as of this printing. If a later version is available by the time you read this, choose that.

Click on your sample research list items one by one. Notice what appears to the right in your Details pane. The Item Type at the top of the Details pane shows you what type of reference you are viewing. Zotero displays beneath that the set of fields you will want to consider completing for that item type.

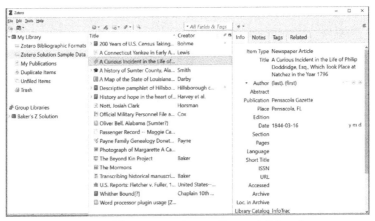

A sample set of data appears in your Research List when you select the sample folder you copied into My Library.

CREATING A RESEARCH CITATION

You enter a new bibliographic citation by clicking on the **New Item** button on the toolbar above the Research List. In the menu it displays, you choose the desired **Item Type**. Depending upon the type you choose, the Info tab will display a targeted set of fields.

The illustrations below show a "Book" type on the left and a "Report" type on the right. While some fields are shared between them, others like the book's ISBN or the report's institution are not.

Some fields will not be included in actual bibliographic citations drawn from the data collected here. The dates added and modified, for example, are in the Details pane and useful for your reference. They are not of value in the bibliographic citation you might draw from this for use in an article you are

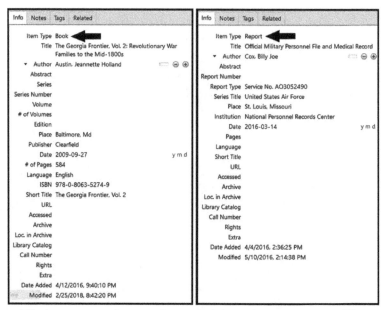

The item type you choose configures the information you may enter. This shows two different views of the Details pane, one a book and the other a report.

writing. In *CMOS* style, the book citation data in this example is formatted this way:

Austin, Jeannette Holland. *The Georgia Frontier*, Vol. 2: Revolutionary War Families to the Mid-1800s. Baltimore, MD: Clearfield, 2009.

The military personnel record, cited with the Report item type yields this citation, in *CMOS* format:

Cox, Billy Joe. "Official Military Personnel File and Medical Record." Service No. [redacted]. United States Air Force. St. Louis, Missouri: National Personnel Records Center, March 14, 2016.

As you begin to collect data in Zotero, it will attempt to save you keystrokes in several data fields. The author, publisher, and place fields, among others, will start to type ahead for you, inserting possible options already used in the system.

Authors, editors, and other key contributors

Most of the fields are self-explanatory, but the author, date, and URL fields have special features. The small arrow to the left of the Author field allows you to change the role of the contributors to the record source you are documenting.

This menu also allows you to rearrange the order of multiple contributors. This will affect their display in your formal citations. The **plus** and **minus** buttons to the right of the names allow you to add or remove contributors. In this example, you have coeditors Jones and Gandrud.

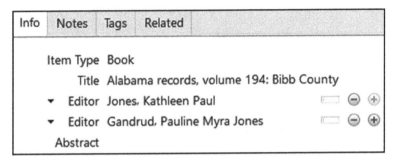

Zotero allows multiple authors, editors, or other participants in the creation of the source record.

The available creator roles change, depending upon the type of citation. If you are capturing the citation information for the Book item type, your options are Author, Contributor, Editor, Series Editor, or Translator. If you use the Book Section item type, you are offered both an Author and a Book Author option, which allows you to make note of a book section authored by someone other than the book's main authors or editors.

Zotero takes the roles you choose for creators in the various item types and creates the proper *CMOS* format for that type of citation. If you are capturing an Interview item type, for example, Zotero will offer you the creator roles of Interview With, Contributor, Interviewer, and Translator.

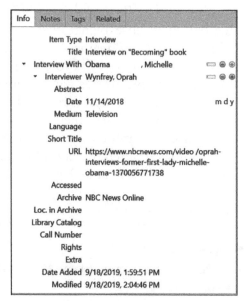

*The Interview item type offers creator roles
of Interviewer and Interview With.*

The Interview With person will become the key creator, and Zotero will insert "interview by" and the Interviewer's name—as the style recommends. The interview with Michelle Obama on NBC News above looks like this:

Obama, Michelle. Interview on "Becoming" book. Interview by Oprah Winfrey. Television. November 14, 2018. NBC News Online. https://www.nbcnews.com/video /oprah-interviews-former-first-lady-michelle-obama-1370056771738

If you are recording a Letter item type, you will need to designate both an Author and a Recipient. Zotero will take these two roles and create the proper citation format of [Author] to [Recipient]. In the section titled "Testing your bibliographic data—Style Preview" in Chapter 12, I will demonstrate how to preview the citations Zotero will create. You will want to experiment in the use of this creator field to optimize your citations.

Date formats

You may enter a date in any of several standard formats, and Zotero will interpret it, as needed. The letters to the right of the date

| Date: 1858-04-17 | y m d |
| Date: 19-Nov-1823 | d m y |

Use the date format you prefer, and Zotero will interpret it.

reveal the interpretation Zotero has made. In the first case above, the date was entered in a year-month-day (y m d) arrangement. The second was formatted with day-month-year (d m y). While these dates would sort badly in alphanumeric order, Zotero knows how to convert the dates behind the scenes, sorting them properly.

In the image below, you see the Research List of your sample data sorted in date order, despite the various date formats used.

Title	Creator	Date
A Map of the State of Louisiana with part of th...	Darby	1816
A Curious Incident in the Life of Philip Doddri...		1844-03-16
The Mormons		March 1851
A history of Sumter County, Alabama, through...	Smith	1988
200 Years of U.S. Census Taking: Population a...	Bohme	1989
A Connecticut Yankee in Early Alabama: Henry...	Lewis	2006-04
Official Military Personnel File and Medical Re...	Cox	3/14/2016
Transcribing historical manuscripts in PDF soft...	Baker	2016-07-13
The Beyond Kin Project	Baker	9 Feb 2018

Zotero supports multiple date formats, allowing for proper sorting.

While Zotero will allow you to type text or date ranges into the date field, it cannot include them in a citation. It will assume that the last episode of four digits that appears anywhere in the date field is the year. It will treat it as a year in the citation. You may get creative with data entry in many Zotero fields, but this one needs to be a specific day, month, and/or year.

The hidden URL button

For a convenient but obscure feature of Zotero, click on the label **URL** beside a web address in a citation. Zotero will open a browser to the stored web address.

URL http://stlcourtrec ords.wustl.edu/index.php
Accessed 9/4/2017

*Click **URL** to go to the stored web address.*

Exercise 1: Add a book

Let's walk through the creation of a research citation record for a published book. We will choose this one: Elizabeth Shown Mills's *Evidence Explained: Citing History Sources from Artifacts to Cyberspace.*

Step 1   Click the **New Item** button on your toolbar and select **Book** from the drop-down list. If it does not appear, click **More** and choose it from the submenu. You will then see the Book item type in the top of the Details pane display.

The New Item button in the top-left corner of the Research List toolbar brings up a menu of item types.

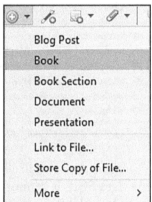

Step 2   Type in the Title: "Evidence explained: citing history sources from artifacts to cyberspace." Tab to the next field.

Step 3   Enter "Mills" in the Author (last) field, tab over, and type "Elizabeth Shown" in the **Author** (first) field.

Step 4   Move down and type "3" in the Edition field; "Baltimore, Maryland" in Place; "Genealogical Publishing

Co." in Publisher; and "2017" in Date. Tab out of the field to save the data.

Zotero will save data each time you exit a field. It has also added the **Date Added** and **Modified** fields for your reference. The first date will not change, always letting you know when you first consulted this source. The second will always let you know the last time you did.

*You choose how much or little information
to gather on a citation.*

There are many fields that can be completed, if needed for your citation or desired for your own records. Not all fields, however, will populate the citations created based on the record. The **Extra**, **Date Added**, and **Modified** fields, for example, are not included in any *CMOS* citations.

QUICK DATA ENTRY OPTIONS

Add item(s) by identifier

Zotero allows you to automate data entry if you have standard identifiers for your sources. On the main workspace toolbar, the **Add Item(s) by** **Identifier** button allows you to take this shortcut. If you enter a book's International Standard Book Number (ISBN), a digital resource's Digital Object Identifier (DOI), or a PubMed Identifier (PMID) for publications in the life sciences, Zotero will pull information into a new citation item for you.

The accuracy of the data pulled in this way depends on the diligence of the person who entered the bibliographic citation into the external databases Zotero consults. You will want to verify that the information came through properly and make any needed corrections.

Exercise 2: Add book using ISBN

Step 1 Type the following ISBN into the field to have Zotero pull in *Evidence Explained* again: **9780806320403**

Step 2 Press **Enter.** That's it! You have added the book.

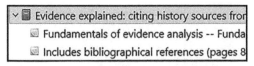

An imported citation brings metadata with it.

You should now have two copies of the Mills book in your Research List. Click on each one to view the data pulled into your Details pane. Assuming nothing has changed in the world's library information or "metadata" since the writing of this book, you will notice that this method pulled in more information than we typed in the manual record. Even better, it will have attached to the citation some notes that describe the book. To see the notes, look for an arrow (>) to the left of the record in the Research List. Click on the arrow and expand what is beneath. The notes have a sticky note icon to the left. When you click on the note title in the Research List, the notes appear in the Details pane. This tool can save you much typing and usually prevent some typographical errors.

If you are adding a citation record to Zotero from a book in your hand, the option above works very well. However, I find myself much more often grabbing source information from online tools, like WorldCat.org, a local library's online catalog, or even Amazon. In Part II, I will introduce you to the feature that first sold me on Zotero as my must-have tool for graduate school. The Zotero Connector allows you to create a robust Zotero citation record with only one click.

Adding Notes

You can create as many notes as you want for any given research source reference. As you do, a list will begin to form in

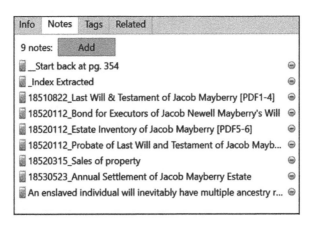

The Notes tab displays the first line of all notes associated with the selected source.

the Notes tab in the Details pane. To create a new note on an existing reference, click **Add**.

As you type a new note, the first line you type will be treated as the note's title. You can find and replace text within a note by using the binoculars on the toolbar. Notes text can be plain or rich-text (formatted) and can interpret and display text formatted by HTML coding.

Zotero's rich-text notes can be formatted with tools on the toolbar. The binoculars allow searching within the text.

Zotero offers basic "rich text" formatting tools, allowing you to bold, italicize, underline, strikethrough, superscript, subscript, color, or highlight text. You can create block quotes, hyperlinks, paragraph styles, varied alignments, bullets, numbering, and indentations. It does not support the assignment of fonts besides those of the designated styles, but rich text in a wide range of fonts can be pasted in from other software tools, like Microsoft Word.

To create a link to a web site from within a note, select the text you want to connect to a web site. Or, put the cursor where you want to create a text link. Click the **Link** button on the format toolbar to bring up the Insert Link dialog box. Enter a URL and the text you wish to Link (if not chosen before coming in). To later follow a link, hold down your control key while clicking on the link. To deactivate a link without deleting the link text, click on the link and choose the "Remove link" button.

Basic text serves well for most notetaking in Zotero, but if you need special formatting, such as tables, you can also create the content in software such as Microsoft Word, and paste it into the note.

The **Edit in a separate window** option that appears at the bottom of the Notes pane allows you to pop the pane out of the larger workspace. Or, you may double-click a displayed item or note in the Details pane to pop out the window. This

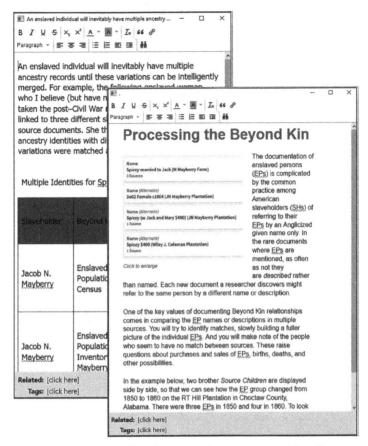

Complex formatting can be pasted into Zotero
from browsers or other software,
like Microsoft Word.

can become very helpful when you are taking notes from another window on your computer. You can narrow the note window beside the window from which you are extracting information. In Chapter 15, I will describe how to apply this to manuscript transcription projects.

You can also create notes that stand alone in your Research List, unconnected to a reference but useful to you. For example, you might wish to create a note with the address and operating hours of an archive. The first line of your freestanding note's contents will appear as its title in the Research List.

DELETING AND RESTORING RESEARCH ITEMS

If you desire to delete a research item completely from your Zotero data, click on *My Library* in your Collections pane to reveal your entire library. Find the item, right-click on it, and choose **Move Item to Trash**. The item will no longer appear in *My Library* but will remain available in Zotero's trash bin, until you choose to empty it.

Zotero's *Trash* can be found toward the bottom of the *My Library* (upper) section of your Collections pane. When you click on it, all records slated for removal will appear in your Research List. If the item deleted was one of multiple attachments and notes beneath a single source reference, the whole reference set will appear. Only the one to be deleted will appear in regular text format. All the other items in that group, including the main reference, will be dimmed out and are not at risk of being deleted.

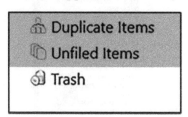

Zotero's Trash holds deleted items awaiting your final choice to empty them permanently.

If you want to restore one of the trash items back to active use in your library, right-click on the specific item and choose **Restore to Library**. The item will be available again for use. If you want to permanently delete one of the items, without emptying the entire trash bin, right-click on the item and click **Delete Item**. To empty the trash completely, right-click on the Trash collection in the Collections pane and click **Empty Trash**.

Keep in mind that the data in your trash bin counts against the storage limits you have in the Zotero cloud. You will want to empty the trash on a regular basis to free up cloud space.

ADJUSTING PANES AND FONT SIZES

You can adjust the visual appearance of Zotero to optimize the workspace for your needs. Go to the User Interface section of Edit—Preferences—General tab to alter your workspace view.

You may find that various tasks you are performing are optimized by changing these settings. You can change them as often as you like.

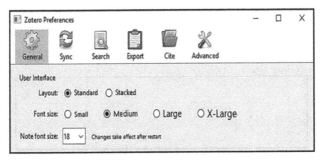

The User Interface preferences reconfigure the workspace view to suit the user.

Zotero Preferences—User Interface

Layout
The Standard view places the Research List and Details panes side by side. The Stacked view places the list above details, with both panes at a maximized width. You may choose to change the layout from time to time, depending on the task at hand.

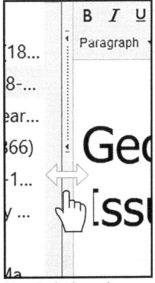

Font size
Four font size options allow you to decide how much information you can see at a time—and how easy it is to see. If you choose a small font, you will see more data—a larger font shows less at a time but is easier to see. This affects all fonts except those in your notes field.

Drag the divider to alter panes.

Note font size

Within any given note, you have substantial control over your font size. Choose an option in the drop-down list or type your own size over the default. The example below shows the notes font set at a very large size, which can be very helpful for those with vision challenges. At the present time, Zotero requires you to close and reopen the program to activate a change in font size for the notes.

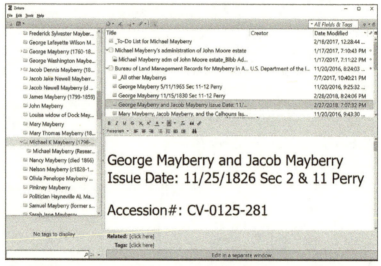

This workspace view now "stacks" the Research List and Details panes on top of each other, rather than side by side. It displays the main font as X-large, the Notes font sized at 48.

Adjusting panes

The size (or even presence) of the workspace panes can also be adjusted, allowing you to determine what data you want to see. When you let your cursor rest on top of the dividing line between panes, a two-way arrow will appear. Click and drag it in the direction you would like to move the dividing line.

You can drag a divider all the way to the left or right edge of the workspace to make an entire pane or set of panes disappear. You can then drag that outer border again to make the pane reappear.

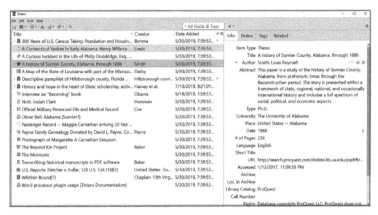

By dragging the divider between the Collections and Research List panes toward the left, the Collections and Tags panes have disappeared, making more room for the Research List and Details.

Creating Tags

In Zotero, "tags" are essentially keyword or subject headings—words that connect a group of your research items together under common themes. You may assign any tag that is of use to you. Click on the **Tags** tab above the Detail pane and choose to **Add**. Once you have created a tag for use on a research item, it will become available from a drop-down list, any time you want to add it to another research item.

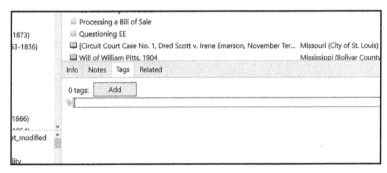

Tags tie your research together thematically.

I use the Tag feature to create for myself an inventory of the books I own. I assign each of them the tag "Personal Library of Donna Cox Baker." As you import research items from external repositories using Zotero Connector (see Chapter 8), some will come with tags already created—often the subject heading metadata created by libraries. You may assign as many to a research item, note, or attachment as you like.

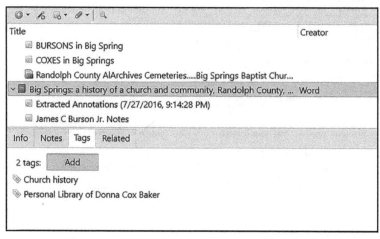

You can assign multiple tags to a single Zotero entry.

Color-coded Tags

You can flag up to nine special tags and automate the color tagging. Right-click on a tag and choose **Assign Color....** Choose a color and click **Set Color**.

Color-code tags to make them quickly identifiable in your Research List.

The tag text will appear bold and in the chosen color in the Tags pane. A position number is associated with the color-coded tag. All future items that are to use the tag can be tagged simply by pressing the number when the item is selected in the Research List. Any research list item assigned the colored tag will appear with a colored square beside it in the Research List.

Automatic Tagging

Research items brought into Zotero using Zotero Connector (see Chapter 8) or by ID number may come in with tags already assigned. If you wish to hide these tags from view, click on the color button in the Tags pane and deselect Show Automatic. You may also choose to delete automatic tags in the library.

IDENTIFYING RELATED RECORDS

The Related records tab in the Details pane allows you to connect specific source records that you want to recall together. For example, you might relate books in a series or a book and all the book reviews you have collected about it. Perhaps you want to "relate" all the correspondence back and forth in a thread. Or you might wish to relate a record of your FOIA request and the response with the information. You add related records in the same way you add tags and notes.

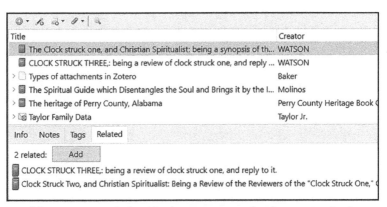

You can create relationships between sources that have a meaning in connection with each other by adding items in the Related tab.

MERGING DUPLICATE ITEMS

You may find at times that you have added the same reference item to Zotero more than once. To proactively find duplicates, click on Duplicate Items in the Collections pane. You can merge the duplicates, if they are the same Item Type. Zotero will guide you through the selection of the desired elements, when they conflict.

Begin by selecting the duplicated records in your Research List. Right-click and choose **Merge Items**. You may experiment by merging the duplicate records of the Mills book we added in earlier exercises. In your Details pane, Zotero will now offer you options to tailor how the merge will take place. First, it asks you to decide which of the selected records should be considered the "master item." Choose the one that is most accurate or has more complete information as your master. Scan down the right side of the merging pane, and you might see small icons of tool bags. Each one represents that conflicting data has been found in that data line. Choose the one you want to keep. When you have made your selections, click the **Merge items** button at the top of the screen.

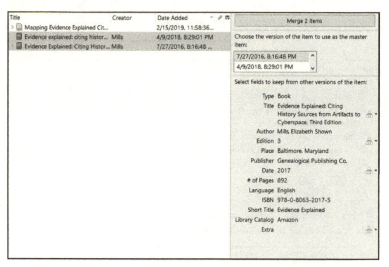

A duplicated reference can be merged, selectively choosing the elements to be retained or discarded.

The multiple items then become one—the most perfect form of the reference. All attachments and notes from the merged items are gathered under the new one.

You will want to exercise caution that the records being merged are truly duplicates and not simply different editions or publications of the same title. Classic titles now in the public domain may be republished by any number of publishers. Page numbering might not be the same. One publisher might use the first edition of the classic and another a later revised edition. But some will be true duplicates—the same record used more than once.

SUMMARY

The creation of research records and notes forms the core function of Zotero as a data storage tool. The citation information is structured while the notes are freeform, making Zotero an excellent blend of the two styles of information gathering. To be useful, of course, you must be able to find the records again. We will begin with the filing system that mimics but dramatically improves upon your old-fashioned filing cabinets.

4: ORGANIZING RESEARCH COLLECTIONS

Zotero's collection structure in the left-most pane of your desktop workspace becomes your filing system—your organizational structure. It allows you to group materials in the way that best serves your research needs. It replaces the file cabinets, binders, and boxes of index cards that we once needed to build our scholarship. And it substantially improves upon the file management that comes standard with most laptops or PCs.

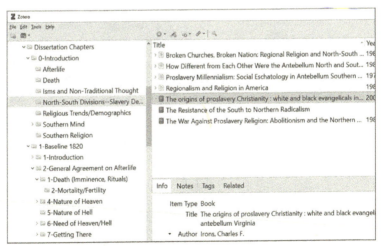

The Collection structure becomes your filing cabinet, binder,
writing outline, or all of these at the same time.

USING ZOTERO COLLECTIONS

A collection is a container for research items that need to be viewed together. It can serve the purpose once handled by a manila folder, binder, file box, or file drawer. It can organize the chapter or the lecture you are writing, replacing the index cards many used to keep. You can make it as small or as large as you need it to be—as simple or as complex.

Zotero sorts its collections in alphabetical order. It handles your files in much the same way we all commonly do in a file cabinet and the way our computer file management systems usually sort files. If you have a set of folders you want to sort in a way other than alphabetically, use a numeral at the start of the collection name.

Collections automatically sort in alphanumeric order. If the order needs to fall in something other than alphabetical order, use numerals to force the order you desire.

As you see in the image, I sorted my dissertation research in order by the chapters and sections I intended to cover, using numbers to make them fall in the desired order. If I changed my mind about the order, I changed the numbers. To change the name of a collection, right-click or double-click on the collection name and type the new text.

If you want to force a collection to the top, begin the name with a symbol (my preference is an underscore). If you want to force one to the absolute end, no matter how many folders you create in between, start the collection name with "zzz" or something similar.

Exercise 3: Create a collection

You have already created your first collection when you copied your sample data to *My Library* in Chapter 2. Rarely, though, will you create your collections by that method. Here is the normal method, organizing your research for a book:

Step 1 Go to *My Library* (top-most item in your Collections pane), right-click, and select **New Collection**. Or, you can use the New Collection button on the toolbar.

Step 2 In the popup window, type "BOOK CHAPTERS," and click **OK**.

Zotero will add the collection above your sample data folder. You can then begin to populate your *BOOK CHAPTERS* folder with subfolders Zotero calls "subcollections."

Exercise 4: Create a subcollection

Subcollections are any folders nested inside of the folders (collections) you have created under *My Library*.

Step 1 Go to your new *BOOK CHAPTERS* collection, right-click, and select **New Subcollection**. Or, you can click on it and use the New Collection button on the toolbar.

Step 2 In the popup window, type "Chapter 1" and click **OK**.

You can repeat this procedure to create more chapters under *BOOK CHAPTERS* or to nest deeper layers of folders under *Chapter 1,* breaking down the material into meaningful sections where you can store applicable research.

For ease in moving around in your growing collection and its subsets, you can collapse subcollections from view. To the left of each folder, you will see an arrow, turned either right (>), indicating that there is a set of folders hidden beneath the one displayed, or downward (∨), which displays any subfolders. Click on the arrow to open and close the containing folder.

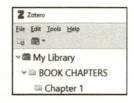

Arrows to the left of subcollection titles can collapse and expand the available contents.

RESEARCH RECORDS INSIDE COLLECTION FOLDERS

Every research record you add to Zotero exists in only one place: *My Library*. As you add the items to the various collections, the research records look and behave as though they reside inside the collection. But the records you see inside a collection are actually virtual links to the main record in *My Library*. Any changes you appear to make to the item in the collection folder, you are making to the main record.

Exercise 5: Testing the virtual links to *My Library*

Let's test out this idea of the "virtual link" that allows a research record to appear to be in multiple folders or collections when it exists only once.

Step 1   Click on *My Library* in your Collections pane. All your current research records will be displayed in the Research List. Click on the item labeled "The Beyond Kin Project." Notice that the Abstract field is empty.

Step 2   In your Collections pane, click on *Zotero Solution Sample Data*. Now click the same entry, "The Beyond Kin

Project," in that list. It appears to be a duplicate of the one you saw in *My Library.*

Step 3   In the Abstract field, type your own name.

Step 4   Click on *My Library* again, and then click on "The Beyond Kin Project." The Abstract field should now have your name in it.

As you can see, the collections appear to have duplicate records. However, only one actually exists—the one in *My Library.* The seeming duplicate in *Zotero Solution Sample Data* is a virtual link to the original record. If you change it here, you are changing the main record.

This is a great benefit over the traditional filing in paper systems and even in most other notetaking software. This allows you to "store" and later find a desired research record in multiple folders, though it exists only once. As you add notes, correct errors, or otherwise improve the record, your changes will appear wherever the record is used.

Exercise 6: Add the record to another folder

Let's say you also want the record discussed above to show up in the new folder you created—your *CHAPTER 1* folder.

Step 1   In the Research List of *My Library,* click and drag "The Beyond Kin Project" over to the *CHAPTER 1* folder. When the folder is highlighted, drop the file there. Notice that "The Beyond Kin Project" record is still sitting in *My Library.*

Step 2   Click on *CHAPTER 1.* The collection now has a single record, also "The Beyond Kin Project." It is a virtual link to the main record, not a separate copy. You can add a virtual link to this record in as many collections or folders as you like.

If you want to remove it from one collection, right-click it there, and choose to **Remove Item from Collection.** If instead, you choose to **Remove Item to Trash,** you will be removing the research record from all locations, including *My*

Library. (It will remain in Zotero's trash bin until you manually choose to empty the trash.)

There may be occasions that you *want* to work on a separate copy of something. In that case, hold down your control key as you drag the item to a new location. You will see a tiny plus (+) sign displayed as your cursor rests above the new folder. When you release the item, a new copy of it will exist in the new folder *and* in *My Library*.

MOVING AND COPYING SUBCOLLECTIONS

The subcollections within a collection folder will organize themselves in alphabetical order, as discussed. But you can move the folder into or out of another folder easily.

Drag the folder you want to move until it is on top of and highlighting the folder where you want it to be. Drop it there, and it will be copied, along with all its contents, and placed in the proper place in the new folder based on its name in alphabetical order.

If you want to move the folder, rather than copying it, drag the item on top of the new collection, but before you drop it, hold down your shift key. Or, if you prefer, drag and drop the copy into the new location, then remove it from the original folder by right-clicking and choosing **Remove item from collection**.

DELETING COLLECTIONS AND SUBCOLLECTIONS

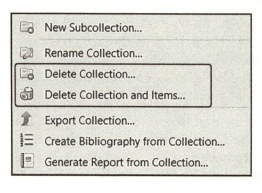

If you want to remove a collection folder from Zotero, you may do it one

You can choose to delete a collection with or without its contents.

of two ways. Right-click the folder and choose one of the following options:

Delete Collection

If you choose this option, Zotero will delete the collection folder and any subcollection folders within it. But the research records you had in the collection folders will continue to exist in *My Library* and in any collections with virtual links to the item. The folders will not be available from Zotero's trash bin.

Delete Collection and Items

This option will delete the selected collection folder, all subcollection folders, and all research records they contained. The folders may not be recovered from the trash, but the research records can be recovered until you empty the trash bin.

SUMMARY

Zotero's collection structure allows you to organize data in the way that works best for you. Even better, it allows you to file something multiple different ways without duplicating the information in reality.

Next, we will look at another feature that mimics old filing systems without the pitfalls. Attachments allow you to store all sorts of documents and files along with the citation records and notes you will take.

5: MANAGING YOUR ATTACHMENTS

Zotero's handling of attachments extends its power and value in many ways. You can store PDFs, text and document files, spreadsheets, images, music, audio, and other types of files. This allows Zotero to replace your file cabinet for all but the collectible photographs, valuable original documents, and certified copies you *should* keep in an original form.

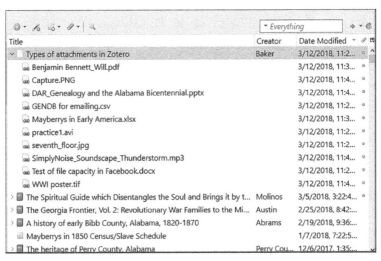

Zotero allows you to link to or embed attachments in numerous file formats, attaching multiple files to a single research record.

The way you set up and manage your attachments can determine the amount of space needed to sync to the Zotero cloud. It will determine whether you will use Zotero to store a copy of all your data or blend Zotero with another storage option. Choices about attachments will also determine the degree to which you can search within your attachments (another remarkable asset of Zotero).

You can attach files to any research record. You can attach as many files as you need to a single research record. The attachments can reside inside Zotero or you can link to them externally on your own hard drive, external drive, or other storage option. You can also have a file standing alone in Zotero as its own record.

BEFORE YOU START ATTACHING

There are a few important things to know about attachments before you start to use them. You will want to make your choices about attachments with long-term storage in mind—and the many variables that long-term *anything* brings to our decisions.

Embedded versus linked attachments

Zotero allows you to embed a copy of your attachments into its database or to create links to them in external locations. While the two options will operate very much the same in your daily use of your research, this choice will affect the size of your Zotero database.

If you choose to link to attachments in external locations, the 300 MB of free cloud space Zotero offers can last a very long time. I have used Zotero for years, accumulating nearly 6,000 research records as of now, with only about 62% of my free Zotero storage used. At the present time, Zotero only counts attachments and web snapshots against your storage allotment—not the space your research citations and notes take up.

I protect my external attachments using cloud storage options I already have in place for other purposes. This ensures that my attachments are being backed up to a location outside my home—something we should all do with our digital resources. This also allows me to access my attachments remotely, even when I am using someone else's computer without Zotero installed.

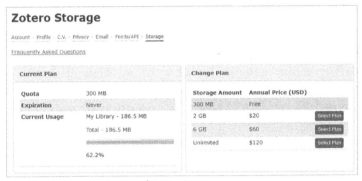

Zotero offers 300 MB of free storage space to sync and access your data remotely.

If you choose instead to store full copies of your attachments in Zotero, syncing everything to the Zotero cloud, be aware that your 300 MB of free storage will run out quickly. A high-resolution image of a single map can be larger than that. Zotero offers 2 GB and 6 GB options, at respectively, $20 and $60 per year. If you will be attaching large files regularly, you will want to choose Zotero's option for unlimited storage, which currently costs $120 per year—a deal you are unlikely to find anywhere else. With unlimited storage, your research records and attachments can be perpetually synced and accessible remotely.

To check your available storage space, login to Zotero.org. Choose **Settings** from the upper-right options, then click **Storage** on the toolbar.

If you can afford to sync your attachments to Zotero's cloud, it will be the ideal arrangement—reducing problems with broken attachment links and offering your research to you, *in full*, when you are away from home. It will also offer funding support to the Corporation for Digital Scholarship, as it improves and maintains Zotero. (I encourage us all to send financial support to Zotero, as we are able.)

Searching the contents of attachments

One feature that makes Zotero an exceptional resource is its ability to search the contents of many attachments—even when you have chosen to link to them externally. Even better, it indexes the contents, making the searches remarkably quick. It can search plain text files and searchable PDFs.

Plain text files are a type of document containing only simple text, with no formatting. You may save them as the "Plain Text" type of document in your word processing software. Or you might create them in a plain text editor like Microsoft Notepad. They typically have a .txt extension, if your computer displays extensions.

More useful for most of us, Zotero can search for a string of text in attached PDF files, if they have a searchable text layer. It is important to distinguish a searchable PDF from one that merely looks like it should be. Some PDFs are actually a snapshot of text. Your eyes can process the letters as words, but a computer simply sees ink spots on a white background, unless an invisible text layer hides behind the image of the page. There is a quick way to tell if your document is readable

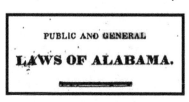

The word "General" has been highlighted when double-clicked, indicating this is a searchable PDF.

as text. Click on a word on the PDF page. If the PDF puts a cursor into the word or selects the word, your PDF should be searchable. If instead, the entire page is highlighted, the page is not searchable.

Some PDF software can create the text layer behind the images of words by a process called Optical Character Recognition, or OCR. OCR is not always perfect in its translation, but even a bad OCR scan can sometimes be helpful in making your document contents findable.

Many other document types—including rich-text documents (like your standard Microsoft Word documents) and spreadsheets—can be saved as searchable PDFs. This will allow you to make most attachments searchable, if desired. If you also want to have access to the document in its native form, you can attach or link to the PDF and then also attach or link to the original file.

Setting a base directory and relative path for linked attachments

If you choose to link to your attachments externally, rather than storing them in Zotero, think carefully about where you store them and how you name them on your hard drive or external drive. As you browse and link to the attachments, you are essentially giving Zotero an address where it can find them—a path. If you later delete, rename, or move the attachment on your drive, Zotero's link will be broken.

You cannot guarantee, even if you are very careful, that you will always be able to keep your attachment files in the same place. Computers become obsolete or damaged. Operating systems are upgraded, forcing unexpected changes. We die and leave our research to descendants. You want to be able to easily move your attachment files from one place to another without breaking the links you have created.

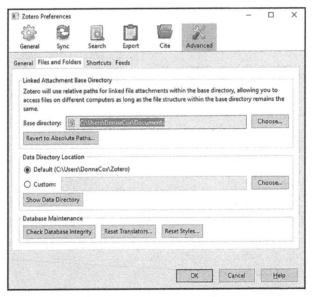

Organize linked attachments in whatever way you wish—so long as they remain in the same path relative to your Base directory.

Zotero offers a way to handle major file movements by allowing you to designate a "base directory," with all your files organized relative to it. You tell Zotero what your base directory is in Preferences—Advanced—Files and Folders. If for any reason you want to move all of your filesto a new location—a new computer, an external hard drive, a cloud location—you can move them all intact to a new base directory and tell Zotero what the new location is.

As you see in the image above, my base directory is

C:\Users\DonnaCox\Documents

Within your base directory, you create the file system that works for your own research. My research happens to be in my family history, so the subfolder that contains my research is labeled "Genealogy." The important thing is to have a filing system for your attachments and to stick to it. Your base directory can change, but everything stored within it must keep its same order and filenames to preserve the links. This creates a "relative path" for Zotero. Your attachment is always in the same place, *relative* to the base directory.

Let's say I have decided to move all my attachments to an external hard drive that is assigned the drive letter D by my computer. Zotero is still looking for all the attachments at the old location, and I could break hundreds or thousands of links by moving the files, without designating a base directory. Let's say I assign a new base directory of:

D:\Zotero\Attachments

I then get my *Genealogy* folder from *C:\Users\DonnaCox\Documents* and copy or move it to *D:\Zotero\Attachments*. My attachments are now all in subfolders of *D:\Zotero\Attachments\Genealogy*. When I click on an attachment link in Zotero, it knows to look in *D:\Zotero\Attachments* rather than *C:\Users\DonnaCox\Documents*. So long as everything within the *Genealogy* folder remains in the same precise structure it already had with the same file names, Zotero will find it.

CREATING FILE ATTACHMENTS

In Zotero, all attachments can be linked to a research citation record. They cannot be linked to a note or another attachment. In your Research List pane, you will right-click on the citation record and choose **Add attachment**. You will then choose one of the following three options:

- Attach link to URI
- Attach stored copy of file
- Attach link to file

Attach link to URI

You might have a reason to link your research record to other dynamic resources—online and otherwise. The Uniform Resource Indicator (URI) link can be a resource name recognizable to certain protocols or it can be the online location of the resource.

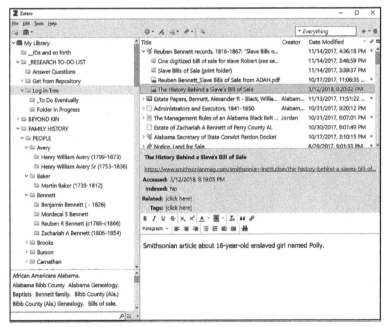

Using the URI link, you can create a meaningful connection to a URL or other resources, using a descriptive title and notes.

For our purposes, most use of this attachment link will be in the form of the Uniform Resource Locator (URL), which is a type of URI that creates a path to the desired resource. In creating a URL, add the link and a meaningful title, which will become the label that Zotero displays in the attachment list for your record.

You already have a URL field in your research citation, which will serve you perfectly well in most cases. But this link allows you to identify multiple resources online that support your research. You can also create a note attached to the URL link, expanding its meaning to you.

In the case of URI links, Zotero will only search what you have typed into the title or the notes. It will not search the contents of the resource to which you are linking. Therefore, you might want to add a few defining terms in the title or notes that will help you to find your way back to this resource.

Exercise 7: Create a URL attachment

Let's say you want to create a link to Elizabeth Shown Mills's website, supporting her book, *Evidence Explained*. You want to attach the link to the citation you have created for the book. Follow these steps:

Step 1   Click on the *Zotero Solution Sample Data* collection in your Collections pane.

Step 2   In your Research List, find the copy of the *Evidence Explained* research record you created, and right-click on it.

Step 3   In the displayed menu, move your cursor to **Add attachments**, which will display a submenu. In the submenu, select **Attach link to URI**.

Step 4   Enter https://www.evidenceexplained.com in the Link field.

Step 5   In the Title field, type "Evidence Explained website with Sample QuickCheck Models" and click **OK.**

Step 6   Double-click on the new link under your *Evidence Explained* record, and you should see the website open for you.

You have created a very convenient way to access the website, but you have also added an element that was missing. By using the words "QuickCheck Model" in the title, you have made this record findable if you search on "QuickCheck," even if you have forgotten the name of the book or author.

Attach stored copy of file

You may attach a copy of a file to your research record so that it becomes a part of Zotero's data. If you are syncing your files to Zotero's online cloud storage, your attachments will be synced, along with your research citation records. See "Copied versus linked attachments" above, for a cautionary discussion of the cloud space needed.

Attach link to file

This option allows you to simply point Zotero to an attachment stored on your computer or another external location. It makes the file quickly accessible from Zotero but keeps it separate from Zotero's main data storage. It will not be synced to Zotero's cloud with the citation records. If you are already syncing your research to cloud storage other than Zotero, you may find this the desirable option. See "Copied versus linked attachments," above, for more information. If you link to a searchable PDF or text file, Zotero will include the text of your attachment in its searches.

The last two attachment options are created in virtually the same way, browsing to find the desired attachment on your hard drive or other device. And from your perspective, they will look and operate almost identically in Zotero. You can only tell them apart by the icon Zotero uses. If you chose **Attach link to file**, there will

be an icon of a document with chain links on top of it. If you chose **Attach stored copy of file**, you will see an icon of a plain document.

The most significant difference between the two will be happening behind the scenes. If you chose **Attach stored copy of file**, your Zotero data increased in size by the disk space that the attachment takes up. And if you are syncing your data to Zotero's cloud, the new file will be taking up some of your space allocation there. If you chose **Attach link to file**, Zotero has only added to its girth a short string of text pointing to a file that already sits on your own device. And when you sync, that small text string, not an entire document, will move to Zotero's cloud.

Exercise 8: Attach a PDF link

To test Zotero's ability to attach documents and to prepare for later exercises, let's pull a PDF from the web to attach to an item in your *Zotero Solution Sample Data* folder.

Step 1   In your web browser, go the following URL: https://gegbound.com/PDFsample.pdf. (This is case-sensitive.)

Step 2   Download the PDF to your computer, either by right-clicking in the screen and selecting **Save As** or by using the Download button on your screen (which probably looks like a down arrow pointing to an underscore). Store it in a place you can remember.

Step 3   In Zotero, select *Zotero Solution Sample Data* folder in the upper Collections pane. Then click on an existing research item labeled **Descriptive Pamphlet of Hillsborough, Florida . . . .**

Step 4   Right-click on the pamphlet item and click **Add Attachment—Attach Link to File**. Find the PDF you just saved to your computer and select it. It will now appear beneath the pamphlet item in your Research List.

DRAGGING AND DROPPING ATTACHMENTS

You can attach files to a Zotero entry by dragging them from your computer's file manager and dropping them on the item in your Research List. By default, this will embed the file into Zotero, adding to its file size. If you wish to create an attachment link, without embedding the file, hold down your <Shift> key before you drop the file. You can drag many files at the same time—useful, if you are moving batches of information into Zotero.

RESTORING BROKEN ATTACHMENT LINKS

Inevitably, you will occasionally find—or even consciously cause—a broken link to an attachment. While the relative path described above in the section titled "Setting a relative path for linked attachments," will eliminate major breakage, you will occasionally move or rename a file, accidentally or on purpose.

    If a link has been broken, you will know it when you attempt to open the attachment and see this message:

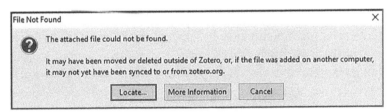

A file that has been renamed or moved will generate this error.
*Click **Locate** to find and reconnect the file.*

    Click **Locate** to search for the missing attachment. Zotero will restore the link when you have located the file. Zotero tells you what it is expecting to find in two ways. First, look in the Details pane, and you will see the filename that was used on the attachment when it was last connected to this Zotero entry. Click on **Locate**, and Zotero will open a file manager window to the folder on your hard drive that held the file when you attached it. Hopefully you will be able to use these clues to find the file where you have moved it or renamed it.

Freestanding files

In most cases, researchers will want files attached or linked to reference entries in Zotero, identifying the source of the file. It is possible, however, to have a file in Zotero without a corresponding reference. You can create this scenario by dragging and dropping a file from your hard drive's file manager into the Research List. Or you can click on the **New Item** button and choose **Link to File** or **Store Copy of File**. If desired, you can have Zotero create a parent reference by right-clicking on the file in your Research List and choosing **Create Parent Item**.

Summary

Attachments are the bulk of what once filled our file cabinets. The simple act of shifting the old paper burden to a digital form on your hard drive offers a great improvement. But by attaching them to Zotero's research records, they become so much more practical than our paper files ever were. Zotero makes them eminently more usable, in no small part because it makes them so much more *findable*. In the next chapter, we will talk about the many ways Zotero helps us find the proverbial "needle in a haystack."

6: Searching, Sorting and Finding Your Research

As our research records grow from hundreds to thousands to potentially tens of thousands, *finding* them again is the key to successful analysis and usefulness. Zotero creates multiple layers of findability, ensuring the best possible success in making your research count.

Basic Sorting

Zotero allows you to sort a selected collection on any of the displayed fields in your research list. If you have selected *My*

Title	Date
John Owen's Journal of His Removal from Virginia to Alabama in 1818	1897
Report of the Commissioner of Education for the Year 1895-96	1897
A Moment with the Players	1897-01-17
Amusements [1897-04-08 Age-Herald]	1897-04-08
Will of Louisa Mayberry	1897-09-23
Land Indenture Mrs. Sally Arnold (Coweta) to Wylie C Lee (Troup)	6 Dec 1897
His View of Women: Rev. A. C. Dixon Says She Has a Powerful Influence on ...	1/6/1898
Centreville	March 8, 1898
Gossip Gathered in Hotel Lobbies	1898-08-12
Countess Starves Herself: A Tragedy in Real Life	1898-12-04
The Manifestation of Spiritualism among the Shakers, 1837–1847	1899

The data has been sorted in order by the Date value.

Library in your collections list, you are sorting your entire collection. Sort the records by clicking on the heading of the column that holds the values you want to sort.

Clicking a column heading a second time will reverse the sort order. Fields with no values will be sorted to the low end of the sorted range.

When sorting the Date field, Zotero will not sort the records in numerical or alphabetical order. It will arrange the material in proper date order, based on its understanding of your date format. Therefore, though your database might include a mixture of date formats—1/5/1854, 5 January 1854, Jan 5, 1854, and 1854-01-05 all being the same date—Zotero knows where they belong in the larger sorted collection.

CHOOSING AND CONTROLLING COLUMNS

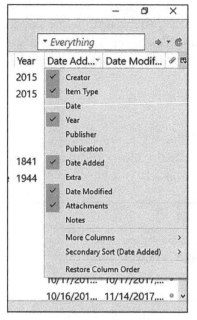

You can choose the columns to display in your research list, which allows you to sort and search with desired precision. Click on the column selection button to the far right of the column headings to choose the fields you want to display.

The most commonly used fields display at the top of the selection list, but many others are available in the **More Columns** option. You are also able to choose a **Secondary Sort** field.

Resize the columns by dragging the thin gray line between the column headings to the right or left. Rearrange the columns by clicking and dragging the heading label, dropping it where you want the column to be.

You may add, resize, and rearrange columns in the Zotero research list.

Exercise 9: Add, arrange, and remove column in research list

To practice these skills, let's sort your research records by their item type. You will make it your first column, sort by it, and then remove it. Click on your *Zotero Solution Sample Data* collection and follow these steps:

Step 1   You need to put the Item Type column into your display. In the top-right corner of your Research List pane, click on the column selection button.

Step 2   Choose **Item Type** from the displayed list.

Step 3   The item type now shows in your list, probably not in the first position. Click and hold the **Item Type** label above the new column and drag it to the left until you drop it on top of the first field—probably your Title. The Item Type should now be your first column.

Step 4   Click on the **Item Type** label to sort your records by Item Type order.

Step 5   To remove the Item Type column, now that you are done with the exercise, click again on your column selection button and choose **Item Type**, this time deselecting it. Or, if you prefer, from the same list, choose **Restore Column Order** to take your entire list back to its original form.

BASIC SEARCHING

Zotero offers a search box above the Research List pane, which gives several options for filtering the search. You do not have to recall exact phrases. Zotero will find any record that contains the terms you enter in the field, regardless of the order of the search terms or the fields in which those terms exist. You have three research options:

Title, Creator, Year

Zotero will search only the three most commonly populated fields in your citation records: the title, the author or creator, and the publication or creation year.

All Fields & Tags

Zotero will seek your search terms in any citation field or in the tags you have assigned.

Zotero's basic search function can look for any of your search terms, filtering the search in basic ways.

Everything

Zotero will search all citation fields, tags, notes, searchable PDFs, and text files for your search terms.

ADVANCED SEARCHING

You can search with greater precision by using Zotero's Advanced Search feature. Access it by clicking on the icon of a magnifying glass on the toolbar.

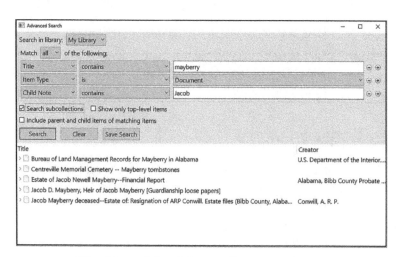

The Advanced Search feature allows you to set up a sophisticated criteria for finding what you need.

You can create multiple criteria, choosing to retrieve records that match any or all your specified criteria. You may seek a specific word or phrase within a specific field. You can have Zotero choose records that do *not* have a specific word or phrase in a specific field. And you can save a search to use again, if helpful.

The search criteria can contain from one to many elements—each further expanding or refining the set of records Zotero will retrieve. You add or remove criteria lines using the minus and plus icons at the end of a displayed line.

Zotero's Advanced Search feature allows you to get very specific in searching for an elusive record.

With each line you add, you will choose the field to search, the evaluation option, and the content you are evaluating in your search.

Field
The field element is chosen from a drop-down list of all available fields in your research records, including collections, tags, and notes.

Evaluation Option
The evaluation option is chosen from a drop-down list that changes, depending on the field you chose in the first element. If you are evaluating the Notes field, for example, your options will be "contains" and "does not contain." The Creator field includes both of those, but adds "is" and "is not," so you can evaluate the entire contents of the field. Date fields will allow you to evaluate before and after criteria, including whether the record contains a date within a certain number of days, months, or years before the current date.

Content
In the content element, you might be presented with a drop-down list or a text box, depending upon the type of field you

are searching. Here, you tell Zotero what information you want it to retrieve (or avoid) in the selected field, as it chooses the records for your review.

You may further refine what Zotero finds and how it displays what it finds by clicking on any of these options:

☑ Search subcollections   ☐ Show only top-level items
☐ Include parent and child items of matching items

Search subcollections
In most cases, you will be searching your entire data set, the *My Library* collection, for which this option has no use. But if you choose a specific collection to search (by selecting "Collection" as your field element on one of your criteria lines), this option will allow you to specify whether the subcollections within that collection will be included.

Show only top-level items
This option controls how the retrieved records will display. If this field is selected, Zotero will show only the research records in which the primary record contains the specified content. It will not pull child records attached to the primary record. If it is not selected, Zotero will display the entire set of research items associated with the matching record—its parent or child records, if available, and any other records attached to its parent. Zotero will display the item that contains the matching record in full resolution. The other items will be faded, but visible.

Include parent and child items of matching items
If this is selected, Zotero treats the parent of a matching child record the same way it treats the child. Both will be displayed in full resolution. If you have selected this and selected the **Show only top-level items** option, only the parent records will be displayed.

Saved searches
If you click the **Save Search** button, Zotero will create an item in your Collections pane, and allow you to give it a name. This

allows you to repeat a search
easily, showing the retrieved records within in the main desktop
view, rather than in the Advanced Search popup window. Your
saved searches will appear as a folder icon with a magnifying
glass in the Collections pane.

Exercise 10: Do an advanced search

Admittedly, we have so little data in Zotero at present that a complex search might seem a waste of
time. But let's do it anyway, in preparation for the
day that you, like me, have 6,000 items in your database—
many entered years ago and no longer remembered well, if at
all. Let's say you have collected hundreds of maps and hundreds of books and articles about maps. You want to pinpoint
actual maps you have of Louisiana in the early nineteenth century. Do the following:

Step 1   Click *My Library* in the Collections pane, which
will open this search to everything in your Zotero
database.

Step 2   Click on the **Advanced Search** icon on the toolbar,
which will bring up the search criteria window.

Step 3   Fill out your Advanced Search window as you see
below—using the plus-sign button to the right of
the first criteria line to add more lines—and click
Search. Zotero will display the one map you have

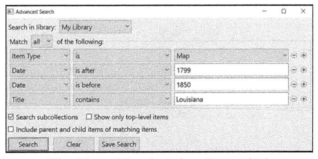

*The Advanced Search window allows multiple
layers of search complexity.*

in your sample data. You can go to that record by double-clicking, but let's say you are going to be collecting a number of these maps and want to be able to repeat the search....

Step 4   To make this search available again later, click the **Save Search** button. Enter a meaningful label like "Early 19th-century LA maps," and click **OK**. You will now have an item toward the bottom of the *My Library* portion of your Collections pane. Click on it at any time to bring your search up in your Research List.

TAGS

You can bring up all of the research items with a particular tag by using the Tag pane in the bottom left corner of your desktop workspace. By default, Zotero displays all available tags. To reduce the options to a particular subset of tags, type a term in the search box at the bottom of the window.

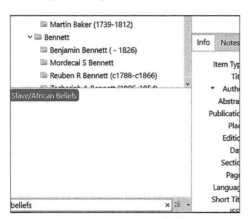

You can filter available tags by entering keywords in the search box.

The dotted icon to the right of the search box allows you to restore the full set of tags if you have isolated to a specific selection. It also allows you to hide "automatic tags," those created when bibliographic research items are imported from your web browser. You may also delete these automatic tags.

SEARCHING AND REPLACING WITHIN A NOTE

Some of the notes you collect in Zotero might be very lengthy. You can find and replace text within a note by clicking on the note and selecting the binoculars icon on the text toolbar in the Details pane. You can replace all occurrences of a specific text string. You can mandate that the case of the text be matched and that the string be a whole word.

Find and replace text within a note using the binocular icon.

LOCATE MENU—LOOKUP ENGINES

Zotero includes "Lookup Engines" that can connect your research records to related entries in available online catalogs and often to full text versions of articles, if you are connected to a participating university server. The Lookup Engines that appear will be determined by what research record you have selected from your own Zotero database.

Some engines are included by default, like CrossRef and Google Scholar. You can also set up a default library for

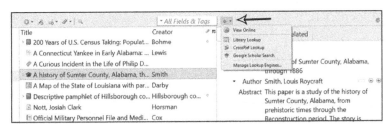

Lookup Engines expand the usefulness of Zotero, connecting it to external library catalogs and databases with full-text articles.

Zotero to use as a catalog lookup for a reference you have entered. The catalog must be online with an "openURL" to make this access work. Some universities have registered their openURLs with Zotero. If you are working on a participating university's network, you may find one in Preferences—Advanced—General by clicking **Search for resolvers.**

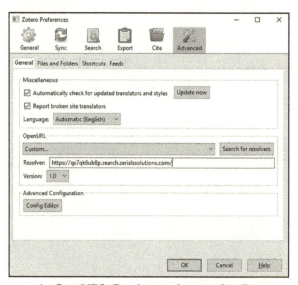

*An OpenURL Resolver can be entered in Zotero
Preferences on the Advanced View—General to set the
Library Lookup.*

You can manually enter an OpenURL on this screen. Zotero maintains a list of many known OpenURLs in its documentation at https://www.zotero.org/support/locate/open-url_resolvers. Many libraries are not listed, but you may find their OpenURL simply by searching their website for the term "OpenURL."

Summary

The ability to retrieve records you have entered becomes vitally important as your collection grows and your memory fades. Zotero offers several ways to find your way back to exactly the source you need.

In the next chapter, we will cover Zotero's ability to import from and export to other bibliographic tools and to offer reports from Zotero based on your Zotero content.

7: IMPORTING, EXPORTING AND REPORTING

Zotero offers several methods of interacting externally with other software or tools. Records can be pulled in, written out, printed and displayed for expanded usefulness. Zotero's timeline reporting feature allows you to analyze data based on timing and sequences of events. This portability of information makes it possible in many cases to move from another bibliographic software tool to Zotero, with less manual effort in getting existing data ready for use. It also protects Zotero users should the software ever become obsolete, providing the path to alternatives, and, of course, this allows you to move Zotero data from one Zotero library to another.

IMPORTING AND EXPORTING FROM OTHER REFERENCE MANAGEMENT TOOLS

Zotero can import and export data to and from many of the major bibliographic software products. You can import an entire research set—whatever has been saved into a compatible importable file—or you may import a single item from the clipboard. You may export your entire library, a subset, or a single record.

Transfers of data in or out should always be done with caution and an attention to the quality of the translation. Many things can go wrong, as data standards change, technology changes, and new operators are keying the data. Test your imports and exports on a few records before you transfer a large number. Make certain that the attachments, notes, and reference data have all come over intact.

Importing an external file

When you want to import an external file, choose **Import** from the File menu. Zotero will present you with one or more file types, depending upon what software you have loaded on your computer. The import option defaults to a single option—A File (BibTeX, RIS file import, Zotero RDF, etc.)—if you have no other bibliographic software on your computer. Zotero's import capabilities include a large number of import options: Zotero RDF, CSL JSON, BibTeX, BibLaTeX, RIS (can be convenient for quick edits between export & import because of its simple structure), Bibliontology RDF, MODS (Metadata Object Description Schema), Endnote XML (best format for exporting from Endnote), Citavi XML (best format for exporting from Citavi), MAB2, MARC, MARCXML, MEDLINE/nbib, OVID Tagged, PubMed XML, RefWorks Tagged (best format for exporting from RefWorks), Web of Science Tagged, Refer/BibIX (generally avoid if any other option is available), XML ContextObject, Unqualified Dublin Core RDF.[1]

Importing from clipboard

Other bibliographic software or reference management tools might have the option of copying a single reference to the clipboard in a chosen reference style. If the style is acceptable to Zotero (see above), you can add it to your database by choosing **Import from Clipboard** from your File menu.

---

[1] Extracted from Zotero's online documentation at https://www.zotero.org/support/kb/importing_standardized_formats on 20 July 2019. Readers are encouraged to check this site for new or discontinued options.

Exporting Zotero records

For exports, depending upon the format, you may choose whether notes, attachments, tags, collections, or journal abbreviations will be included with the bibliographic data, and the character encoding you prefer. You can export as a single record, selection, or the entire library. You may choose to export your library as a Zotero RDF file, to save as a backup. It can be a comma-separated value (CSV) file. It can export to EndNote, RefWorks, Evernote, and Wikipedia. Many other options expand the number of products that can receive Zotero data.

*The CSV format will export your records
with comma-separated values.*

CREATING REPORTS

Generating Zotero item reports

Zotero will create a report of a single record or a group of them from your Research List. Select the record or records you want to include, right-click, and choose **Generate Report from Items**.

Zotero will create a web-based report, neatly organizing the reference information—leaving out fields you did not com-

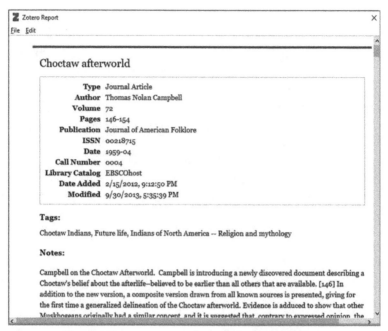

Zotero will create a report from any item or set of items.

plete. It includes your notes and adds a reference to any attachments that are available. When you have selected multiple items, they will be sorted in alphabetical order by the title.

You can select the report text and paste it into a word processing document, in order to have further control over it. Or you can print it to PDF. Its native form is a web page, and you can save it as that.

Creating a color-coded timeline

Zotero can work from your entire database or any subset to create a timeline of sources. This can be helpful in a field like history to demonstrate the evolution of reporting on an event. In literary criticism, use it to analyze the changing arc of a writer's interests or style. In almost any field of study, it offers a scholar a visual look at how a subject of study has changed over time.

Open *My Library*, then go to Tools—Create Timeline to visualize a timeline. If you selected a group of records, only those are included. Otherwise, Zotero will select any record in the active collection.

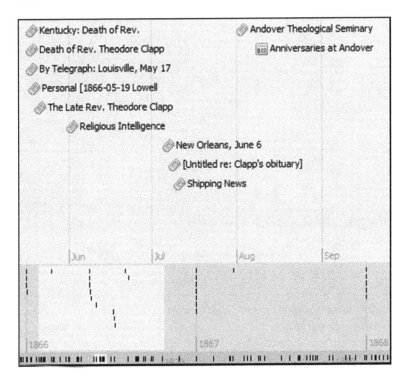

The titles of sources appear in the timeline with
links to the Zotero record.

You can move around in the timeline by dragging the gray bar. The speed with which it moves depends on whether your displayed "bands" are lengthy periods, like decades, or small ones, like days. Enter a year in Jump to Year to move quickly to a place in the timeline.

All sources for a particular time will appear in the timeline with their titles. You can click on the title and open the record in your database.

Other fields further refine and expand the analytical value of the view. The Filter field allows you to isolate the view to a subset of records containing the text you type into the field. The Highlight fields allow you to highlight with four different colors any records that contain a specific text string. Both help you to do a visual analysis of trends.

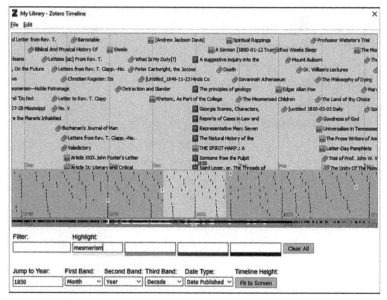

The timeline displays sources by date in their publication year, allowing various types of analysis. Color coding helps to isolate particular records.

You can choose Edit—Copy to put an image of the timeline into your clipboard to be pasted elsewhere. You can also print the visible portion of the timeline to a printer or PDF file. While Zotero offers a save option to save to a webpage, it saves only the timeline structure, not the data.

Pasting bibliographic references or notes externally

You can quickly and simply copy and paste bibliographic references from Zotero to other environments. Perhaps a colleague or student has asked you to send a reference you mentioned in conversation or in class. Or someone has asked you for the set of references behind a statement you made in a talk. You can paste a single reference or a set of them, using the style of your choice. Select the reference or references from your Research List and right-click, choosing **Create bibliography from item**.

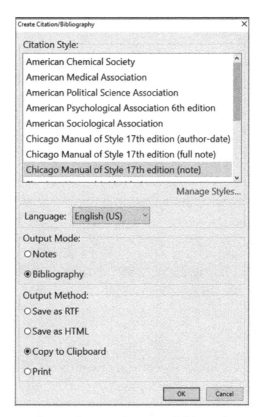

Copy and paste a footnote or bibliographic entry for any Zotero item or set of items.

Select your preferred style (this will usually be defaulting to what you normally use) and language. Choose whether you are formatting a footnote or bibliography format and select **Copy to Clipboard**. Click **OK**, then go to the external environment. Paste from the clipboard. A selection of the first five items from your sample data, with bibliography format chosen, pastes here in this way:

Baker, Donna Cox. "The Beyond Kin Project." Power Point presented at the Annie Veal Brooks African American Symposium, Milledgeville, GA, February 9, 2018.
———. "Transcribing Historical Manuscripts in PDF Software." *The Golden Egg Genealogist* (blog), July 13, 2016. http://gegbound.com/transcribing-historical-manuscripts-pdf-software/.

Bohme, Frederick G. *200 Years of U.S. Census Taking: Population and Housing Questions, 1790-1990*. U.S. Department of Commerce, Bureau of the Census, 1989.

Chaplain 10th Virginia Cavalry. *Whither Bound[?]*. Parrish & Willingham. Confederate Imprints. Raleigh, NC: s.n., 1861. https://archive-org.libdata.lib.ua.edu/details/whither-bound00rale.

Cox, Billy Joe. "Official Military Personnel File and Medical Record." Service No. [redacted]. United States Air Force. St. Louis, Missouri: National Personnel Records Center, March 14, 2016.

A single item, with the Notes option selected, appears like this:

"A Curious Incident in the Life of Philip Doddridge, Esq., Which Took Place at Natchez in the Year 1796," *Pensacola Gazette*, March 16, 1844.

SUMMARY

The import, export, and reporting features of Zotero expand the power of the product to serve research and to offer it to others. These are the last major features available in Zotero as standard. Several other tools were created as Add-ons and have become standard to its operations for most users. The next part will describe these options.

PART II:

ZOTERO ADD-ONS

Zotero is "open source" software, allowing its own personnel or other organizations or individuals to build extra features to expand the application. Of the numerous available "add-ons," I will describe the three most essential ones I have used for years with great success.

The first two, "Zotero Connector" and "Zotero Word Processor Plug-in," are supported by Zotero. The other one, "ZotFile," programmed and supported by Joscha Legewie, offers excellent tools for enhancing the use of PDFs.

You can find many other tools available on Zotero's website, though they are not created or supported by Zotero. You need to be aware that you use them at your own risk, and many may be well worth the risk. Some require programming knowledge to implement. You can examine the list at

https://www.zotero.org/support/plugins

8: Zotero Connectors & Instant Data Entry

The Zotero Connector first hooked me on the Zotero product, making it unbeatable in my opinion. The connector is a plug-in for use in your Internet browser, to capture bibliographic data from a web page, entering it into Zotero with the push of a button. With thousands of bibliographic citations to enter while working on my dissertation, this saved me hundreds of hours and much aggravation, as it continues to do.

Installing Zotero connector

Zotero offers connectors to Chrome, Firefox, and Safari web browsers, specifically, and also has a "bookmarklet" for any other browser, smartphone, or tablet.[*] The Zotero Connectors can all be downloaded from the Zotero website by choosing **Install Browser Connector** from your Tools menu. In recent updates, Zotero offers a link upon your initial installation, encouraging you to install the connector, so you might already have it installed on your computer.

I use the Chrome browser, so the instructions here will be for Chrome. If you prefer another browser, Zotero offers wider options.

---

[*] The operation of bookmarklets will vary, depending upon the environment. Search Zotero's online forums for details about your own device and software.

For Chrome, select **Install Zotero Connector for Chrome**. For all other browsers, select **Zotero Connectors for other browsers** and follow Zotero's instructions for your browser. If you are operating from within Chrome as you do this, you will see a notification about adding the extension to the browser environment. Choose **Add extension**.

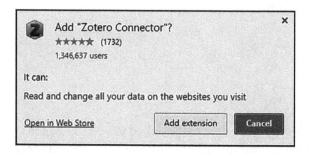

Your Chrome browser will give you a second notice that the extension has been added, pointing to a tiny icon that now appears at the top line of your browser window, just to the right of your URL field. The icon will change shapes, depending upon what type of information Zotero perceives to be displayed on the screen.

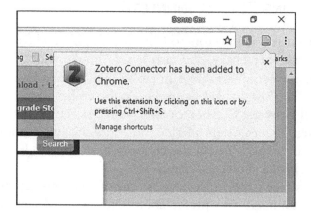

If you are on an informational website—one that *is* the content, not a citation of content elsewhere—it will look like a computer screen. If you are looking at a book advertisement on Amazon, it will look like a book. Let your cursor rest on top of it, and if you see the words "Save to Zotero," you have located the proper icon.

This icon will become your method to populate your Zotero research records with citation information someone *else* had to type. You will love the work it saves.

USING THE ZOTERO CONNECTOR

Your Zotero software must be open in the background for Zotero Connector to operate properly. You can use Zotero Connector on any page displayed in the browser you chose to enable with the add-on. Zotero attempts to interpret the type of web page it is on, in order to draw the most useful data from it.

I find it most valuable and accurate in capturing items from library catalogs online. It also captures book data from Amazon. And if it does not see bibliographic data within the displayed website (or if the site's metadata is masked as private), Zotero Connector assumes that you want to capture the displayed site as a webpage, and it draws the proper bibliographic information for that.

Zotero Connector will extract the information and create a new Zotero record. The record will always be displayed in *My Library*, but it will copy a link to the record in the Zotero subcollection active at the time the connector button is pushed on the webpage.

Exercise 11: Create a record using Zotero Connector

Let's say you need a book from the Tuscaloosa Public Library. You believe it will be of value to your research, and you are going to go ahead and put its citation in Zotero—primed and ready for that day when you actually get the book and take notes. Do the following:

Step 1   In Zotero, click on your *CHAPTER 1* collection.

Step 2   In your web browser, open the Tuscaloosa Public Library online catalog at www.tuscaloosa-library.org.

Step 3   In the library's search box, type "Early Settlers of Pickens County" and click **Search**.

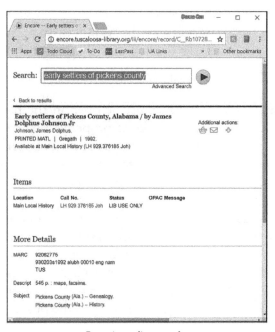

Item in online catalog

Step 4   The catalog will bring up a book by James Dolphus Johnson Jr. Click on it to display the full record. (If by chance this record is no longer in the catalog by the time of this printing, pick another book.)

Step 5   With the book record displayed on the screen, click on the Zotero Connector icon in the top right corner, which will most likely appear as a blue book icon. Zotero will display a message to let you know the record is being written into its database.

Step 6   Go back to Zotero. The new record should be in your *CHAPTER 1* collection, having pulled the record from the Tuscaloosa Public Library database.

Thanks to the wonders of "metadata," Zotero knew exactly what information to put in each field. You will always want to check behind this process, however, because the person who cataloged the information in the library catalog might have done so inaccurately or incompletely.

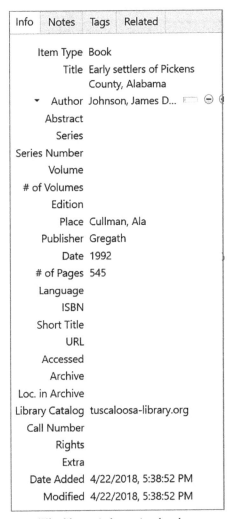

The library information has been extracted to Zotero.

Many of you will find this tool especially helpful in populating Zotero with your old research, starting with your book library. You can find the books in an online catalog like World-Cat and let the catalog do a lot of your work for you.

Web snapshots

When you first set up Zotero, the system marked a default value in Edit—Preferences—General to include a snapshot of any website that is captured through Zotero Connector:

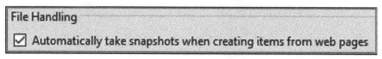

Snapshot default setup.

With this default activated, Zotero will take a screenshot of the webpage and attach it to the reference record. This can be very helpful, if the website disappears or is changed later. But it also will take up space in your data and can quickly use up the free cloud sync storage that Zotero offers you.

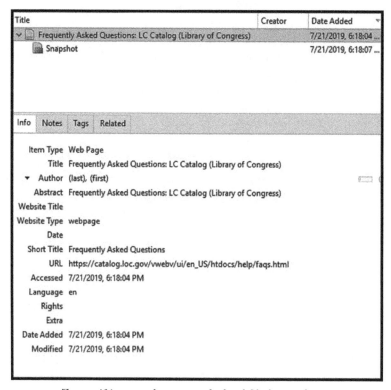

Zotero, if instructed, captures the html file for a web page as it was at the moment cited.

If you are trying to preserve that space, but want the security of the snapshot, you can simply choose to save the web page to your separate cloud space and then create a link from Zotero. If that is your preferred method, deselect the default value in your preferences.

If you find that Zotero has been creating snapshots and you want to free up the space, you can delete the attachment. But keep in mind that it will continue to take up space in your trash bin until you empty it.

Summary

Though it is technically an "add-on," you should consider Zotero Connector an essential part of your Zotero work. It will magnify your effectiveness at research and remove the worst of the aggravation. We will cover another amazing time saver, ZotFile, next.

9: ZotFile & Advanced PDF Management

As you find and collect new research treasures, you will often have to set things aside to read later. You need a reading list that keeps you on top of what you have not yet done. And as you read those things, you will want to highlight passages and take notes that end up in Zotero. ZotFile allows you to create what I am calling a "reading stack" from your Zotero collection and, if needed, to transport it to your tablet or other reading device. When you get done reading, it lets you turn your PDF notes and highlights into searchable, usable text in Zotero.

ZotFile has been designed and maintained for many years by Joscha Legewie of New York. He charges nothing at present, only asking users to consider much-deserved donations to the continued development. He offers more complete documentation online than I will attempt here. You can find his notes at zotfile.com.

Installing ZotFile

Do the following to install the ZotFile add-on:

Step 1   Go to **zotfile.com** online. [Note: the instructions here are valid as of 11/20/2019. If you have problems, check for new instructions on the zotfile.com website.]

Step 2 Click **Download** from the left sidebar. A file will download to your computer.

Step 3 Go to Zotero on your desktop. From the main menu, choose **Tools—Add-ons.**

Step 4 In the Extensions view, click on the gear icon in the top-right corner. From the menu, click **Install add-on from file**.

Step 5 Browse to your Downloads folder on your computer and double-click the ZotFile program that has just been downloaded (or open the new file that is displayed at the bottom of your screen if your computer shows downloads there).

Step 6 A security window will open. Choose the **ZotFile** item in the window, then click **Install Now.**

Step 7 ZotFile will appear in the list of Extensions you have installed. Click **Restart Now** to close and reopen Zotero to activate ZotFile.

Once you have installed ZotFile, a new menu option called **ZotFile Preferences** will appear under **Tools** on your Zotero menu. You will quickly see that ZotFile offers many complex options—far more than we will attempt to cover here.

We will cover the ones I have used with the greatest value to academic research. And we will only alter the preferences that serve those features. We will focus on ZotFile's ability to store your reading stack in a convenient way and its ability to extract your annotations (highlights and comments), creating notes from them in Zotero.

However, if you find that you need to investigate Zot-File's other options, in order to deal with your particular hardware configuration or file organization, you can read the add-on's documentation online at zotfile.com.

CREATING A ZOTFILE READING STACK

As you begin to find PDF documents you want to cite and access through Zotero, you will often be working quickly. You may find yourself at a library or archive, rapidly gathering documents that you will only have time to read with care later. Eventually, when you have some time to read, you can dig into the documents that await. ZotFile helps you to manage this, putting the PDF where you can access it, and making sure it winds up safely back in its proper place in Zotero.

ZotFile checks the PDF out of Zotero for you, much like checking out a library book. It knows what you have checked out, and ensures you know the PDF is there if you find your way back to the citation record in Zotero before you have read and returned the PDF.

Let's begin by setting up ZotFile's preferences to create a reading stack for you to use on your laptop, tablet, or smartphone. Determine where you want to store your reading stack. If you have an iPad or other tablet, for example, you likely have set up a cloud folder where you can pick up and store documents you want to share between your tablet and your computer. The same could be true of reading files on your smartphone (though keep in mind that PDFs might not be easily readable on a phone-sized screen). If you are going to use your laptop to do your reading, and it is the same computer you use to do your Zotero work, you can pick any spot that is convenient for you on your hard drive.

To set up your ZotFile preferences, do the following:

Step 1 Open your ZotFile Preferences from your Tools menu and click on the **Tablet Settings** tab.

Step 2 In the Location of Files on Tablet section, type the path to your reading stack folder in the Base Folder.

Step 3 Deselect **Rename files when they are sent to the tablet**. Make sure all other settings on this tab are as they appear in the diagram.

Tablet Settings tab in ZotFile Preferences

To send a PDF file from your Zotero collection to your reading stack, find it in the Zotero Research List, right-click on it, select **Manage Attachments**, then choose to **Send to Tablet**. Zotero will put a copy of the PDF into the directory you selected in your preferences above.

If you prefer, ZotFile will create a subfolder within whatever directory you established as your reading stack in the preferences. It will name the subfolder the name of the collection in which the PDF is displayed in Zotero. You will see this option at the bottom of your list of options when you right-click on the PDF.

You can use your computer's file management tool to get to your reading stack. Or, open your ZotFile preferences to the Tablet Settings tab again and choose to **Show Folder** beside the path you set up as your storage location. If you are using a tablet or smartphone, you will want to link through your device to the location.

Exercise 12: Send a PDF to the reading stack

Let's experiment with the PDF we pulled into Zotero in Exercise 8 in Chapter 5. These instructions will assume you are reading the PDF on your laptop, rather than a tablet or smartphone, but you can use any of the options for the reading. Follow these instructions to send the PDF to your reading stack:

Step 1   In your Collections pane, click on *Zotero Solution Sample Data* to display your sample research items.

Step 2   Find the research item labeled "Descriptive pamphlet of Hillsborough county, Florida." Beneath that (you might need to expand the arrow beside the entry) you should have a PDF titled "PDFsample.pdf." Right-click on the PDF and select **Manage Attachments—Send to Tablet**.

Step 3   Open the directory you set as your "Location of Files on Tablet: Base Folder" in your ZotFile Preferences. (You can go through your computer's file management system or go back to ZotFile Preferences—Tablet Settings and choose **Show Folder**.)

Step 4   Open the PDF.

This is how you can create your reading stack, either reading your collected materials on your computer or accessing them through your tablet or smartphone. You may keep Zotero open and take notes on your reading as you go. But ZotFile offers a way to eliminate a lot of that work.

EXTRACTING ANNOTATIONS FROM PDFS

Most PDF software allows you to add comments and to highlight text, if your document has recognizable text, as opposed to a graphic image. ZotFile will convert highlighted or commented text (annotations) into notes.

An annotated file is returned to Zotero by right-clicking on the original PDF in the Zotero research list and choosing

Manage Attachments—Get from Tablet. If the default values were accepted in your ZotFile Preferences, ZotFile will bring the copy back into Zotero, adding the extension "_annotated" to distinguish it from the original. It will create a note called "Extracted Annotations," which contains the contents of any comments or highlighted text, identifying the page number for each.

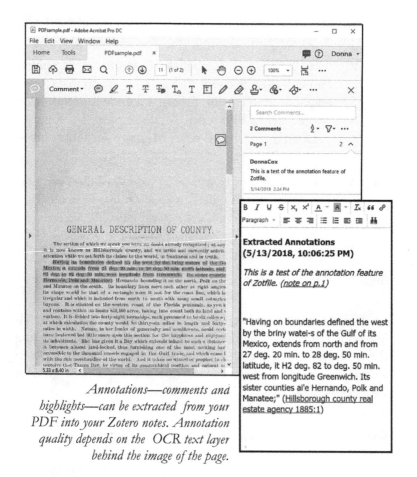

Annotations—comments and highlights—can be extracted from your PDF into your Zotero notes. Annotation quality depends on the OCR text layer behind the image of the page.

Exercise 13: Extracting annotations from your PDF

Picking up where we left off in the last exercise, we will annotate the PDF copy sent out of Zotero by ZotFile. We will then retrieve it into Zotero with the notes extracted.

Step 1   Open your PDF file, if you closed it after the last exercise.

Step 2   Add comments and highlight a few sentences from the PDF, then close this annotated document and save it.

Step 3   In Zotero, right-click on the original PDF, called **PDFsample**. Choose **Manage Attachments—Get from Tablet**. ZotFile will draw back into Zotero the copy of the file you have annotated, applying the text "_annotated" to the end of its title. Both the original and the annotated copy will remain unless you decide to get rid of one.

Step 4   ZotFile should have created a new note item under your Hillsborough County pamphlet citation. Click to open this new note titled **Extracted Annotations**. In your Details pane, you will see all of the text you highlighted or typed into comments in the PDF.

Our sample PDF in this exercise was fully embedded in Zotero—not connected externally by a link. Therefore, both copies of the PDF after this exercise are embedded in Zotero, being synced, and taking up space. On the other hand, if you had done this exercise on a PDF that resided externally and was linked into Zotero, ZotFile would treat the copy the same way—as a linked file, with the copy residing in the same directory where you put the first file.

If you prefer to keep only one copy of the PDF—the one with the annotations, you can set your ZotFile Preferences to do this. In your preferences, go to the **Tablet Settings**. Deselect the option that says **Save copy of annotated file with**

suffix. The new copy of the PDF, with your annotations, will replace the original file, carrying the same name.

Extracting annotations without sending the PDF to the stack

ZotFile will allow you to extract annotations from PDFs you have not sent to the reading stack. Right-click on the PDF in your research list, choosing **Manage Attachments—Extract Annotations**. ZotFile will create a note called "Extracted Annotations," just as it does when you send a PDF to the stack. If you are dealing with PDFs as you encounter them, rather than saving them up for later reading or processing, this method will likely be preferred.

SUMMARY

While ZotFile is a bit more complex at the start than many Zotero features, it offers a service of great value in doing scholarly research. It also becomes quite simple to operate once you have installed it and chosen your options.

Next, we turn our attention to an add-on designed to create your endnotes or footnotes and bibliography in a word processor. This tool can dramatically reduce the time and effort required to format scholarly writing for publication or course credit.

10: WORD PROCESSING & PAINLESS CITATIONS

In graduate school, I had to write numerous research papers, a thesis, and finally a dissertation. The history field required adherence to a mammoth publishing style guide called the *Chicago Manual of Style*. I call this one-thousand-plus pages of rules *CMOS* (SEE-moss). Once Zotero entered the picture, though, I lost my dread of citations and bibliographies. They wrote themselves.

In professional research, we find ourselves in need of similar help for the writing of formal articles, books, and research reports. Zotero's add-ons (interchangeably called "add-ins") for Word for Windows, Google Docs, OpenOffice, LibreOffice, and other environments will take much pain out of it for anyone using standard publishing styles.

INSTALLING THE WORD PROCESSING ADD-ON

If you are on Zotero 5 or later, Zotero installed the necessary software when you installed or upgraded to it. For our instructional purposes here, we will use Microsoft Word for Windows as the model, but the functions should be similar or include documentation.

Setting up your word processing options

To properly set up this add-on, go to Edit—Preferences and click **Cite** on the toolbar. The Style Manager offers you access to the 9,500-plus publishing styles that have been set up in Zotero. New ones are being developed continuously.

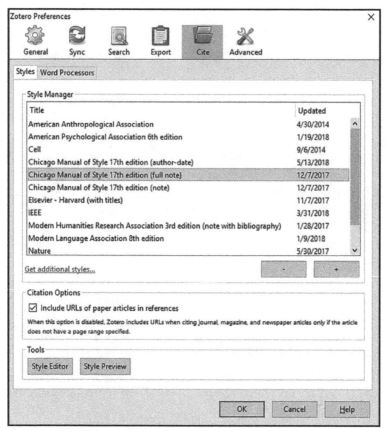

In your word processor add-on options, you select your desired style for any documents you will be creating.

Unless you have a specific style requirement other than *CMOS*, select **Chicago Manual of Style 17th edition (full note)**—or a newer version, if available. Select **Include URLs of paper articles in references**, also, unless you are writing for a publication that does not want URLs included in citations or bibliographies.

Next, check to ensure Zotero has installed the word-processor add-ons. Click on the **Word Processors** tab beneath the toolbar. If it tells you that yours is not installed, click on the appropriate button. You will come back here if your word processing software ever accidentally breaks the link to Zotero and press the button to reinstall it. When everything is set up, click **OK** to save your options.

For Google Docs, the add-on is installed when you set up Zotero Connector in Chrome. For other word processing environments, not displayed here, search the Zotero.org documentation for available plug-ins and instructions.

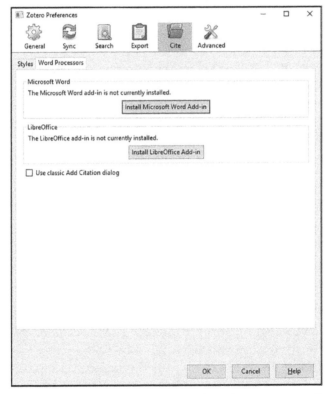

On your Preferences—Cite view, you have the option to install your word processor's add-on, if it is not already installed.

ZOTERO TOOLS IN YOUR WORD PROCESSOR

You have research stored in Zotero now and your word processing add-on set up. Next, we will start using the add-on in your word processing software. Open that software, create a new blank document, and examine the tools Zotero has installed for you.

The Zotero menu option opens the tools needed to retrieve Zotero research citations.

In Word for Windows, you should see a Zotero tab on your menu bar, probably the last item, unless you have added other customizations to your software. Click on the tab, and a set of tools will appear beneath the menu bar.

With these tools, you will be able to pull citation data from Zotero and format it as footnotes or endnotes. When you have created these notes, you can then use the tools to create a bibliography. The data you pull in is "dynamic." Let's say you find later that you had something incorrect in Zotero. You correct it in Zotero, then you can refresh your document, replacing the incorrect information throughout the entire document with your corrected Zotero information.

Document preferences

Before you begin to work with your new document, you will want to make sure you have set your preferences. Click on **Document Preferences** on your Zotero add-on toolbar. You are offered the following options:

Citation Style
> Choose one of the available publishing styles. This defaults to the one we chose in Zotero: *CMOS*.

Language
> Choose the language your citations will use.

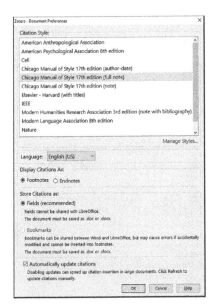

Display Citation As
Choose whether your citations are to be footnotes or endnotes. A footnote appears at the bottom of the page containing the text the note supports. An endnote appears at the end of a chapter, report, or book—gathered with all the other citations.

Store Citation As
Choose whether you want the citation to be stored as a field or a bookmark. In most cases, you will want to choose **Field**. This creates the dynamic reference in your word processor, which can be updated as information changes in Zotero. If you plan to move your document over to LibreOffice at any point, you will need to choose **Bookmark**. (Test thoroughly before transferring any document with Zotero citations to another word processing tool. Transfer a *copy*, not the original.)

Automatically Update Citations
Choose this if you want your document to pull in changes from Zotero automatically that would alter citations you have entered. As your document grows large, you might prefer to turn this off, to speed up your entry of new citations. If you deselect this option, you will want to click **Refresh** on the Zotero toolbar occasionally to manually update all fields in your document.

CREATING CITATIONS IN YOUR DOCUMENT

The Zotero add-on for Word makes citation creation remarkably easy. When you have written something that requires a citation, you click the **Add/Edit Citation** icon to bring up a bar that interfaces with your Zotero database. You can find the desired Zotero record by typing in enough text to point Zotero to it. Zotero will bring up a list of all research records matching your search text. You will highlight the source record, then click **<Enter>** to create the citation.

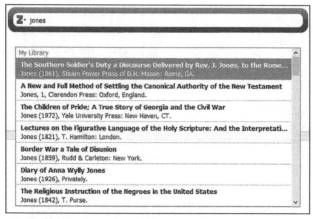

*Type a string of text from your source's author or title
to bring it into the drop-down list for selection.*

Exercise 14: Create a citation

Let's experiment with adding a citation to your empty document.

Step 1 Type this sentence into your document: "The case was decided in the late nineteenth century."

Step 2 Click on the Zotero menu option to display your tools.

Step 3 Click **Add/Edit Citation** to create your citation.

Step 4 Type "Fletcher" and select this option:

U.S. Reports: Fletcher v. Fuller, 120 U.S. 534 (1887).
United States--Supreme Court (1886), 22.

Click **<Enter>**. The Zotero add-on will insert a superscripted number at the spot where you were in the document.

¹ United States--Supreme Court, "U.S. Reports: Fletcher v. Fuller, 120 U.S. 534 (1887)," 120 US 534 Property Law § Volume 120 (1886), https://www.loc.gov/item/usrep120534/.

It will create a footnote at the bottom of your page that looks like the one above.

ADDING MULTIPLE ZOTERO CITATIONS

You will often find that you need several Zotero records to support a statement you have made in your document. To create multiple citations within a single footnote, click **Add/Edit Citations** from your Zotero menu. Type in the search string for the first record you want to cite, and select the correct one from Zotero's list. Then, rather than clicking **<Enter>**, type another search string. Repeat this until all citations are included for this one footnote.

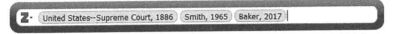

Enter multiple search strings to create a footnote with more than one citation.

Zotero will separate the citations by a semicolon, as is common practice for the *CMOS* style, looking like this:

¹ United States--Supreme Court, "U.S. Reports: Fletcher v. Fuller, 120 U.S. 534 (1887)," 120 US 534 Property Law § Volume 120 (1886), https://www.loc.gov/item/usrep120534/; Winston Smith, "Early History of Demopolis," *Alabama Review* 18, no. 3 (April 1965): 83–91; Donna Cox Baker, "The Beyond Kin Project: Documenting Enslaved Populations," *AGS Magazine* 49 (Spring/Summer 2017) (2017): 2–9.

SUBSEQUENT MENTIONS

The Zotero add-on follows the selected style's rules for subsequent mentions of a source already cited. A style might use the Latin term "ibid." to reflect that a citation is being repeated from the one just above it. It might use an abbreviated form of a citation if the same source appears a second time within the same chapter. For *CMOS*, the abbreviated forms can use a shortened version of a source title, if you chose to enter one in the Short Title field in the Zotero Detail form.

EDITING A CITATION

As you create citations, you might find that you have pulled the incorrect one, or that you need to add further information to make the citation complete. Or you may realize that you had the information incorrect in Zotero to begin with. You may easily correct all of them, by one of several methods. Let's take them one by one.

Choosing a different Zotero record

If you chose the wrong Zotero record, you can do one of two things. First, you can simply delete the superscripted number in your text, which will delete the footnote or endnote. Then you go through the steps again to add a new record. Or, you can click anywhere in the footnote, and click **Add/Edit Citation** on your Zotero menu.

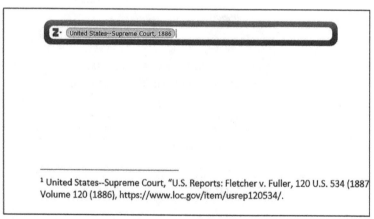

Z▾   United States--Supreme Court, 1886

[1] United States--Supreme Court, "U.S. Reports: Fletcher v. Fuller, 120 U.S. 534 (1887 Volume 120 (1886), https://www.loc.gov/item/usrep120534/.

*Put your cursor in the footnote and click the **Add/Edit Citation** icon in your Zotero menu to edit the citation.*

The Zotero Add-on will bring up the Zotero bar again, with the selected record displayed. Backspace to remove the citation you chose, then type in text to find the one you prefer.

Adding a page number to your citation

Many of your Zotero records will contain general bibliographic information, but you will want to get more specific as you cite a specific fact you draw from the source. You will want to identify the page number, most commonly. You can add a page number as you are selecting your Zotero record, by typing a comma, a space, then your page number, and clicking the **<Enter>** key.

Type a comma and number to add a page number to your citation.

The Add-on will only accept a number after the comma. If you type letters, it will assume you want to add a second citation. When you complete your number, and press **<Enter>**, it will place the number in the appropriate page number format for your citation's style and item type.

If you decide to add a page number after you have already created the citation, click in the citation text and click the **Add/Edit Citation** button on your Zotero menu. The selection bar will reappear with your citation field displayed. Type the comma and page number after it, and Zotero will fold it into the field with a period after it. Click **<Enter>** to reformat the citation with the page number in it.

[1] United States--Supreme Court, "U.S. Reports: Fletcher v. Fuller, 120 U.S. 534 (1887)," 120 US 534 Property Law § Volume 120 (1886), 22, https://www.loc.gov/item/usrep120534/.

You may also expedite your footnote entry by typing in the search text, a comma, space, and page number *before* selecting

Expedite your data entry with a search string and page number.

your Zotero footnote. When you make your selection, the page number will be embedded.

Adding further detail to a citation

You might want to add explanatory text about your source— or further detail about how to locate the record. Click on the record name in the Zotero bar, and a small menu will appear, offering you the chance to add a page number, prefix, and suffix to the existing Zotero record. It also allows you to suppress the inclusion of the author's name, if desired.

A word of caution

As long as the citation remains linked to Zotero, you cannot simply type into the footnote Zotero has created. You can add text at the end of the citation—*after* the Zotero-created text. If you make a change *to or within* the text that Zotero created, then attempt to do a formal edit or refresh the data, Zotero will bring up a warning message.

If you choose to keep the text you have added by answering **Yes**, the connection to Zotero will be invalidated. If you later make changes to this bibliographic reference within the Zotero database, it will not be updated in your document. If you answer **No**, Zotero will remove the text you have added.

To add text that can remain without invalidating the Zotero link, either use the prefix or suffix option described above, or put your cursor behind the closing punctuation of the footnote and type there. Zotero will allow that text to

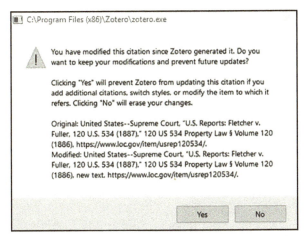

The choice to embed or alter text within a footnote or endnote that Zotero has created will render the link with Zotero invalid, if you choose to keep it.

remain. The bold text below demonstrates where you can add text.

¹ United States--Supreme Court, "U.S. Reports: Fletcher v. Fuller, 120 U.S. 534 (1887)," 120 US 534 Property Law § Volume 120 (1886), https://www.loc.gov/item/usrep120534/. **Here is where you may type further information for your readers.**

Keep in mind that you will not be able to insert commentary between multiple citations that have been combined into a complex footnote, except by using the prefix and suffix fields. You can add any desired commentary on the collection of citations at the end of the paragraph, as you see in the bold text above.

CREATING A BIBLIOGRAPHY

Zotero's Add-on in Word offers a very simple way to create a bibliography of all sources cited within the document. Go to the spot in the document where you want the bibliography to appear. Click on the **Add/Edit Bibliography** button on the Zotero toolbar, and the bibliography will be inserted at the spot. Zotero will format it according to your chosen style.

When you have all citations in place in your manuscript and are ready to do a final polish, you can sever the links to

Zotero. First, make a copy of the document—always keeping a Zotero-linked copy, should you make future variations of the document. To break the links, choose **Unlink Citations** from the Zotero toolbar. Any editing you do to the Zotero-generated citations and bibliography will now remain intact.

Zotero will create a bibliography for you at the desired spot in your document.

SUMMARY

Scholars use *CMOS* or another established style regularly in their writing but can still find the style rules difficult to recall. This add-on allows Word and Zotero to do the recalling for you. You can concentrate on sparkling writing and worry-free scholarly research.

We will discuss methods for adapting Zotero's capabilities to your environment and needs for that worry-free research in the next chapter.

PART III:

APPLYING ZOTERO
IN YOUR ENVIRONMENT

Congratulations on having gotten through the introductory material. Now we get to the most essential thing you came here for: Zotero as applied to scholarly research. As I am sure you realize, there will never be a comprehensive book on a subject like this. There are simply too many variables—too many fields of research. But the essential elements are here—the beginnings upon which you can build.

11: ORGANIZING YOUR FILING SYSTEM

Filing systems are very personal concoctions. First in school and later in my business, writing, publishing, history, and genealogy careers, I have evaluated many an organizational system. I learned from some and adapted what worked. For many, I wondered, "What were they thinking?" Some are needlessly complex. Some are hopelessly inefficient. They are complex and inefficient to *me*. But here's the beauty of it. It's up to you. What works for you?

As you ponder that, you need to also look ahead and ask what you will need for the long term. What system can grow with you? Will your research continue for years to come and be rendered into many different output formats—a dissertation, lectures, articles, books, and more? A decade down the road, will you be able to harness the resources you gathered in graduate school for reuse?

Whatever organizational system you embrace or develop, Zotero can almost certainly be tailored to support it. This chapter offers my counsel on certain key practices to maximize your Zotero organizational experience. I also describe my own filing system for family history research, in case it is of help to you, conceptually, as you design your own knowledge management structure.

THE MAIN THING: ONE SYSTEM FOR ALL

Organizing your Zotero system successfully depends on following this one rule: mimic the filing system you use outside of Zotero. If you have found that a complex alphanumeric coding system is your preferred method of filing research, then mimic it in Zotero.

Apply a consistent filing system every place you are filing materials, if possible. Apply it in Zotero, on your computer hard drive, in the cloud, and in your paper files (if you continue to keep paper). You might not have control over source organization in databases you share with others. But keep the rest of it consistent, and you will minimize your research storage and retrieval hassles.

This consistency is most important when you are linking to files outside of Zotero. If something happens to break the link between a Zotero record and a file on your computer, you will have the easiest time reconnecting the link if you have filed both items in a similar fashion.

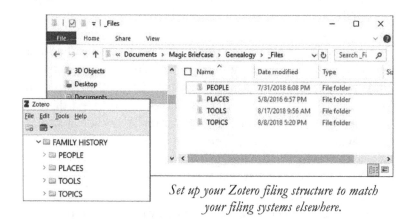

Set up your Zotero filing structure to match your filing systems elsewhere.

DESIGNING YOUR FILING SYSTEM

If you are not yet committed to a system, let me recommend a few things. First, consider that you might find yourself using Zotero for things other than your scholarly research, and make room for that. At the very least, you might need to separate personal files from your scholarly research.

Personal files

Zotero can hold a widely creative variety of information of use to you personally. It can hold articles about a stock you are following. You can capture recipes. You might want to keep up with your prescriptions and the paint colors on your house walls. You might even want to keep your daily journal in it, as I do.

An important thing to know as you plan your Zotero structure is this: Zotero is open source. It is not designed to be a high-security data storage option. Your work will be as secure as your computer is. If your computer is sitting on your desk at work, and others can get to it, your Zotero data is available.

Clearly then, consider what you are willing for anyone with access to see. I would not, under any circumstances, store passwords, credit card numbers, or other IDs in Zotero.

There is a way to create separate libraries for your Zotero work, with personal or confidential material only available on your home computer. I discuss this later in the chapter. I like to have Zotero as my complete "catch all" solution, though. I like to open it at the start of my work day and drop everything into that I want to store, *without* having to open and close two (or more) different Zotero databases.

Scholarly research files

If you are doing scholarly research in more than one area, you might want to create a major folder for each kind. Let's say you are a professor of 20th century European history by day and a first-century Bible scholar by night. The two areas of research are not likely to share sources and may need very different filing structures. It makes sense to separate them.

On the other hand, you might find there are certain types of references that serve both fields of interest. Let's say you are collecting articles about using Zotero. Perhaps you are gathering some about improving your academic writing skills. Maybe you are researching the type of computer you need for your work.

Think about where this sort of research-related information might be stored. Think about where you would look for it again, the next time you have a similar reference item to store.

TWO-PRONGED RESEARCH FILING

One of Zotero's greatest values to researchers lies in its ability to store the same information in many different folders without physically duplicating the data. For scholars, this is especially helpful in that you may find yourself using the same information many different times—in your book, several articles, and a lecture.

Also, your research often begins in a broad search and study—long before you know how you are going to organize your book or article or lecture. While you will eventually want to gather research under chapters or major talking points, you must have a place to keep the data for the long haul—for all purposes.

For this reason, I recommend that you take a two-pronged approach to filing your research data. Create a permanent collection structure that accumulates everything you know about a subject or even about your whole field of interest. Store this data topically.

Then create collections for any projects that borrow from that body of research. This could be the book project, talk, articles, or other uses. Organize these collections into chapters or major points. As you are formulating your thoughts, in preparation for writing the chapters or major points, drag and drop the references from your topical folders to these. The information can then be found in either place.

For my dissertation, it worked like this. I knew that I wanted to study afterlife beliefs in the antebellum U.S. South. And I had picked up enough in my doctoral reading to know that ideas like Spiritualism, Mesmerism, Universalism and the sciences were flowing through and being debated at the time. I had no idea yet how I was going to organize my dissertation.

My first layer of research was very general, and topics began to emerge. I had a folder for Mesmerism, one for Universalism, and so forth. As I read the primary literature, the

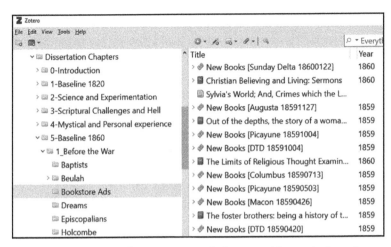

Organize Zotero's folder structure to mimic your writing project's outline, using numbers in the topic titles to create the proper order.

topics expanded to include slave beliefs, pedobaptism, ghosts, and many others. Each collection became a basket to gather what I was finding—and eventually to yield the ideas that would form the dissertation. And if a source addressed multiple topics of interest to me, I dragged it into multiple folders.

When I got ready to work on the dissertation, I created collections to represent each chapter and then subcollections beneath each to represent sections within the chapter—essentially creating my project outline. Reviewing the topical material I had been collecting over time, I began to drag items into the place they appeared to fit in the dissertation-in-the-making. Then, as I wrote the dissertation, I reviewed the material I had gathered about each topic or line of thought.

In this way, the first of the two prongs shapes the second—topics yielding project structure. And the second borrows from the first to yield the scholarship.

GETTING SPECIFIC WITH YOUR TOPICAL RESEARCH

We are hardly uniform in our research organization needs. We are working on vastly different fields of study. And even those of us in similar fields might be looking at very different subjects. Each will need to build the system that works best for the need at hand. But I do recommend getting to a system of some sort as rapidly as you can. The longer you go with a haphazard approach to organization, the harder it will be to make sense of what you have found—if you can recall it at all.

My general field of history is possibly very different than yours, especially if you are in the sciences. But perhaps looking at the structure that has come to work for me will give you an idea of how to *think* about your data, even if it is not the right structure for you.

Those doing biographical, family, or local history research—where names and places proliferate—may find this very simple organizational method helpful for the first prong of research. You can tweak the model, based on your specific needs.

Just about everything I might need to file related to my current family and plantation history work can be categorized under one of the following headings:

PEOPLE
PLACES
TOOLS
TOPICS

Organizing people

I am dealing with large numbers of people in my research—often people with the same names. I organize them first by surname, then by given name with birth and death years, if known. Surname variants can be included in the label, like "Cox/Coxe." If the variants create confusion in alphabetical order, say "Cox/Koch," you can use the variants, then create an empty folder labeled, "Koch (see Cox)."

I place women in the families of their birth, when known, since it is likely to be the most stable surname. If I only know a woman's given name and her attachment to her husband's family, I place her temporarily in a folder inside her husband's folder. I label it something like, "Penelope wife of John (1821

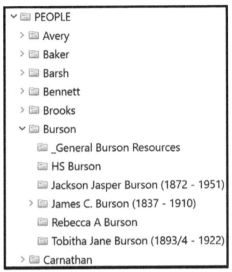

*People are organized by their birth
surname, then their given name
and birth and death years.*

-)." When I find her maiden name, she will be moved to her birth family's surname.

Keep in mind that changing a folder label on my hard drive will break Zotero's link to the attachments within the folder. So, when I discover the missing birth year or move the woman to her birth family's folder, I immediately reconnect any broken attachments in the folder. The good news is this: since I am using the same file structure everywhere I am filing information, I can easily find the material in Zotero in a folder corresponding to where I stored it on my hard drive. I simply click on any broken attachments, select **Locate**, then find the new hard drive location.

When I find a document that names many different family members within a surname, I create a folder on my hard drive called "_General [Surname] Resources," rather than make multiple copies of the attachment. It exists only once on my hard drive. Meanwhile, all the people named in it have a link to that same document created in Zotero.

Also, some documents will name multiple surnames I am researching. On my hard drive, above the surnames, I have a file labeled "_Multifamily Resources." I store such documents there and, again, link all applicable people in my Zotero files to the one document.

The most important thing, as I label my PEOPLE folders, is to make sure I distinguish people with similar names. I might want to add a county or some other distinguishing word, like "doctor" or "preacher," for people with the same name. I choose the thing that will help me to know on sight which Tom Smith folder is the one I want to use.

My goal is to keep the rules to a minimum, but to have a system that is clear enough to rapidly retrieve exactly what I seek. I want no more and no less than that.

Places

For resources about a locality, I store materials in my PLACES folder. Most of my work at this stage is in the United States, which will likely always be the major research area. So, I organize my U.S. locations directly under PLACES, without forcing another layer above them called "United States." For other nations I am researching, I work

Organize places by major political entities, with smaller subsets nested inside. States hold counties, which hold cities, which hold institutions.

within a subfolder of PLACES labeled "_International." The underscore at the beginning of the label forces it to the top of the sorted folders.

In dealing with U.S. localities, I organize first by state, then county, then city. Where useful, I go even more specific, with a folder for a church or cemetery or school within the locality. I only go to this level of detail when I have a number of resources about a single institution.

Places, like women's names, can change names, boundaries, and even sovereigns over time. I do not stress too much about how to organize these bouncing details. I just make sure I leave myself a breadcrumb trail. Let's say I have chosen to store a document under its name at the time the document was created: "New Merkle." When I am looking for that document ten years from now, I might think I stored it in the name of the locality now, "Cahaba Heights." I can choose to name the two folders "New Merkle (now Cahaba Heights)" and "Cahaba Heights (formerly New Merkle)," if I think that would be helpful. Or I can put both names in the notes for the document so that a search helps me find it. Or, I might choose to create a note within the locality folder that gives some of its history—creating the needed breadcrumb trail in that document.

Tools

In the TOOLS folder I collect information about tools that will help me in my research. Zotero is such a tool, and I want to grab articles that teach me how to use it optimally. I can store software instructions here and warranties, receipts, and correspondence of value.

I also keep wish lists here, when I have an idea how a tool developer might improve a product. I can write up my "hacks" and workarounds to the product's limitations. I can make note of reported bugs, and store notices of what is supposed to be added to future versions of the product.

It is especially helpful for the evaluation of tools I do not yet have. I can collect articles and surveys that give me the perspective of others on one product category or another.

Topics

In genealogy, I find myself researching all sorts of topics like the laws regarding unwed mothers in 1850s Heard County, Georgia, or the influenza epidemic of 1919 in Birmingham, Alabama. I might open the newsletter of a local genealogy society and see a great article I want to save, about ICD codes on death certificates. I will want to consult that again, so I drop it into a TOPICS folder called "Death certificates."

I might want to write a blog post about how to determine what the weather was like in a particular place and time. I will drop relevant notes into a folder called "Weather," until I have enough to write a meaningful post.

MORE ON THE BREADCRUMB TRAIL

Anyone engaged in research knows how quickly you can get lost in the weeds. The filing described above and the searching described in Chapter 6 are critical parts of finding your way back. It is also important as you gather material in Zotero to ask yourself, "How will I find this again?" Have you filed it in all the most likely places you would search for it? And this is even more critical: Have you embedded the search terms you might use, if you are looking for it again?

Let this become a standard refrain in your head. Before you let go of a new piece of research evidence, ask yourself, "Have I left myself a breadcrumb trail?"

CREATING A SEPARATE ZOTERO PROFILE

Thanks to the multilayered nature of Zotero, you might never need to create a separate Zotero profile. A separate profile creates a completely different set of Zotero data, and syncs to a different account. Typically, you cannot run both versions of Zotero simultaneously, though your system might be configured to do so—if you have the technical skill. I use this feature when I am teaching Zotero or writing about it and in need of images of Zotero as the reader will see it before data is entered.

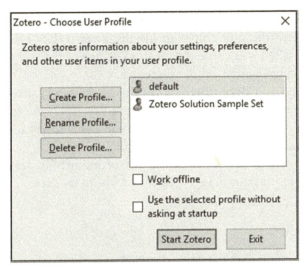

When multiple profiles exist, Zotero launches with this dialog box. Once you have opened the desired profile, you must log out and relaunch Zotero to select another.

Zotero's online documentation gives the instructions for creating separate profiles for the various operating systems. See https://www.zotero.org/support/kb/multiple_profiles.

For Windows, first close out of Zotero. Go to the Windows Run command by typing **Run** into the Cortana search bar. Then type **"C:\Program Files (x86)\Zotero\zotero.exe" -P**, including the quotation marks in your entry, and press <Enter>.* Windows will display this access window:

The default profile is your normal working environment in Zotero. Choose **Create Profile** and click **Next**. Give your new profile a name and choose **Finish**. Zotero creates the new profile.

After this, any time you open Zotero, you will be offered the window above, to choose which version you want to use. The first time you open the new profile, it will still be pointing to the data of the original profile, which is set at the Data Directory Location in your preferences. Go to Edit—Preferences—Advanced, then choose the **Files and Folders** tab. Next to the Data Directory Location, click **Choose**. You will

---

* This assumes you installed Zotero to its default location on your hard drive. If you used a different location, alter the path accordingly.

need to create a directory in which to store your new profile's data. Place the new folder inside the Zotero data folder that opened when you chose the location. Zotero will force a restart after you have changed the directory.

When you open the new profile again, it will present the same screen you were given when you first opened Zotero, allowing you to set things up. You will need to create a new Zotero account and set up the syncing.

If you later choose to delete the second profile, you will be given an option to delete it with or without its data.

SUMMARY

You can be confident that you will encounter exceptions to every rule you create for yourself in your filing system. Rather than seeking a perfect system, which will fail you, make sure you leave yourself clues to find your way back to any document. Your Zotero search capabilities can find things in the most obscure places, so long as you have left a few keywords in your record that you will remember.

As you begin to create records in Zotero, the filing system will get simpler with use. A complexity arises when a single source has information on many things related to your research—a census record, for example. Do you set it up as one source or many in Zotero? We address that next.

12: ONE SOURCE RECORD OR MANY: A CHOICE

As you prepare to capture your research information and citations, you will be faced with choices. A single major source might contain information about numerous things in your research. Would you make the major source a single Zotero reference, or would each different subject of interest within that major source become its own record? You can do either or both. The important thing is to think about what you need to be able to draw from Zotero. Pick the most efficient method for your needs in any given case.

A SOURCE RECORD WITH MANY NOTES

Let's say your research is for a biography. You want to talk about the person's ancestry and their descendants and find a history of the town in which they all lived. If it is a small town and the subject's family in multiple intermarried family lines lived there for many generations, you will likely find family on many pages in the book. There are several ways to document such a situation in Zotero.

Certainly, you will want a traditional bibliographic entry for the published book—one place where you document it as a whole. But you have a decision to make about handling all the references to the extended family.

If you want to capture a single bibliographic reference for a book, as entered in the image above, the formatted citation would appear like this:

Word, Mary Florence Arthur. *Big Springs: A History of a Church and Community, Randolph County, Alabama.* LaGrange, GA: Family Tree, 1986.

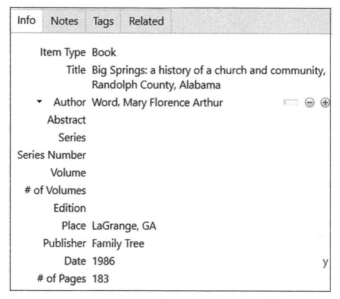

A single published book might hold many references to family members in multiple branches of a family.

All notes under one reference

The simplest way to handle this situation is to create the book reference (or website or other major source) only once in Zotero and have all your related notes beneath it. If the major source mentions multiple branches of your biographical subject's family, you could create a note per surname. If you are citing references in a book, be certain you include the page number in the notes, so that you can easily find the reference again, and so that you can cite the source in published citations.

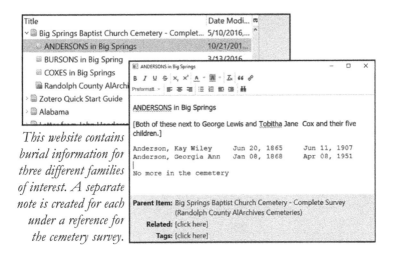

This website contains burial information for three different families of interest. A separate note is created for each under a reference for the cemetery survey.

Using book sections for finer detail

You might find it useful to break up the notes or your citations into finer detail. Perhaps a single note per surname has become too bulky.

Maybe you want to create separate notes per person. You can create Zotero references with the Book Section item type and create section titles like "[Bursons in Eller's Heard County history]." There is no chapter in Lynda Eller's book that is about the Burson family, but I can create this citation and collect everything she mentions about Bursons in the book. I encase the section title in brackets as a reminder that this was not a formal chapter title.

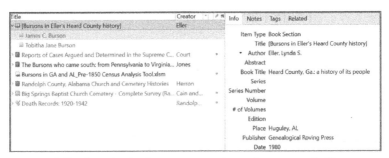

A "book section" reference type can be used to segment bulky references in a single source, in this case segmenting by surname.

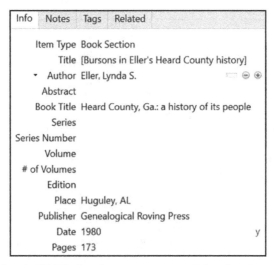

Encasing the Title in brackets serves as a reminder that there was no chapter heading with that title. It serves instead as a way to gather like materials in a book.

The notes added to this reference can be labeled by your subject's ancestors—collecting information about each separately. You will still have the full book citation information but will have a copy per surname.

As another example, the entire book might be about a single family. Each chapter is about a generation. You might want to create multiple Zotero references as "book sections," chapter by chapter rather than (or in addition to) the full book. The title of the chapter becomes the book section title. You can then break up your notes by generation, and your notes might be about specific people in that generation.

A local history book might include a labeled section about one or several of your subject's family branches. Or it might include a biography section about a specific ancestor. You could use a book section to deal with this piece of the main source separately.

When using book sections, the section title becomes the title that displays in your Research List pane. If you create a bibliographic reference, it includes the section title. A book section labeled "Caswell" in Lynda Eller's history of Heard County, Georgia, appears like this:

Eller, Lynda S. "Caswell." In *Heard County, Ga.: A History of Its People*,
173. Huguley, AL: Genealogical Roving Press, 1980.

This works well for formally labeled book sections, like
"Caswell" above. If you are using a book section as an informal
way of breaking up a large mass of information, though—as in
the example of "[Bursons in Eller's Heard County history]"
above—you would not use the section title in a formal bibliographic reference. You will be reminded to pull the section title
out when you see the bracketed reference, looking like this:

Eller, Lynda S. "[Bursons in Eller's Heard County history]." In *Heard
County, Ga.: A History of Its People*, 173. Huguley, AL: Genealogical Roving Press, 1980.

A CASE STUDY

There will be occasions in which you will find it useful to make
a separate bibliographic entry for a number of items that you
might have incorporated under a single citation. While you
could create a single entry for a newspaper, for example, then
put the date and title of the articles in your notes, it can be
useful to make each newspaper article its own entry. The newspaper articles, being dated, can create a timeline of events.

My search for information on Choctaw County Sheriff Ja-
cob Mayberry's name brought 110 hits in Alabama newspapers
in Newspapers.com. The
town apparently took note
every time his daughters held
a party. They reported it the
night his wife accidentally set
the house on fire while cook-
ing dinner. These are great
nuggets of family life, and I am lucky to have them.

—Misses, Hale and Drummond,
two very estimable young ladies of
York, are visiting the family of Mr.
J. D. Mayberry in this place.

Choctaw Herald *July 24, 1890.*

His name also appeared in the paper, though, every time
property was seized and every time they listed the "County Directory" of local officials. Many of these articles have little to
offer me in their specifics. Still, rather than cite the name of the
newspaper only once in Zotero, I chose to make each article

its own entry in Zotero. By creating them in Zotero separately, I am creating a timeline of Mayberry's activities over nearly five decades. I know where he was and what counties were choosing to report on him at any given time.

Announcements [Party of youngsters at home of JD May...	1890-04-03	Choctaw Herald
Minutes of the Democratic Convention, held at Butler, C...	1890-05-29	Choctaw Herald
County Directory	1890-07-23	Choctaw Advocate
Notice. [Visit of Misses Hale and Drummond]	1890-07-24	Choctaw Herald
County Directory	1890-08-20	Choctaw Advocate
> Commissioner's Court	1890-08-27	Choctaw Advocate
> Gaining Ground	1890-08-27	Choctaw Advocate
> County Directory	1890-09-03	Choctaw Advocate
> County Convention	1890-09-04	Choctaw Herald
> [n.t.--J.D. Mayberry and State Alliance]	1890-10-16	Choctaw Herald

Dated articles can create a timeline of a person's whereabouts and activities.

TESTING YOUR BIBLIOGRAPHIC DATA—STYLE PREVIEW

Some of your work to document sources will be experimental in the beginning. There will be records that do not fit established models, and you will need to document them as well as possible. Follow this procedure to see how your citation will look as you make various changes to your Zotero entry:

Step 1   Size your Zotero workspace to cover only half of your monitor.

Step 2   Find and click on your record in the Research List.

Step 3   From the Main Menu, choose **Edit—Preferences**, and click on the **Cite** button.

Step 4   Be sure the **Styles** tab is selected. In the Style Manager, click on **Chicago Manual of Style 17ᵗʰ edition (full note)** and click the **Style Preview** button near the bottom of your window.

Step 5   Position the new window so that it is visible beside your Zotero main window. Click **Refresh** to bring your record's bibliographic formats into view. Scroll to show the *CMOS* formats.

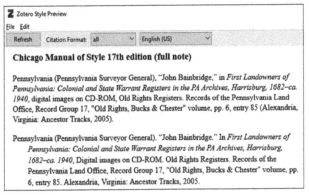

*The Zotero Style Preview shows you what your
record will look like when formatted as a
footnote or bibliographic reference.*

Step 6 If the style is not satisfactory to your needs—something is missing or will be confusing in retrospect—adjust your Zotero record.

Step 7 Refresh the format window and review it again. Keep doing this until you have the format that will work best for you.

SUMMARY

You may use several different strategies for dealing with a bulk of research findings within a single major source. In any case, you need to ask yourself how you will find the information again. If you plan to extract citations from Zotero for use in published materials, ask yourself how the method you have chosen will work. You will want to minimize duplication of effort without losing benefits later in your projects.

In the next chapter, we will talk about other ways to maximize the effectiveness of your research efforts. Zotero can be used as a research planning tool, helping you remember the questions not yet answered and know exactly what to look for when a research trip materializes.

13: Research Planning

Each scholarly field has its own methods and standards for planning and carrying out research. In the sciences rigid methods and standards tend to apply, with precise measures of proof. Other fields, like the arts and humanities, tend to be more fluid and even creative. Whatever your field of study and specific research projects, Zotero can aid you in planning your research and keeping up with your status.

Logging your research

If your scholarly field has specific logs or reports to be kept to document research activities, you may consider creating links to them in Zotero. This keeps both your research and any support tools for it available through the same portal.

Also, given Zotero's ability to store the same item in multiple folders, you can organize your logs in more than one way. Let's say that you create a report or log for each experiment you do in a scientific research project. You might want one folder that holds all logs or reports. But you might want the report or log for a specific experiment to also show up in the folder with other research materials you created or gathered for that experiment. Further, you might want a folder that separates completed reports from those in progress or in need of review.

In a field like history, documentation of your specific research goals and findings while on a research trip to an archive can be very helpful in preventing duplication of effort or, worse, failure to get what you came for. A historian might thoroughly search through a set of records in an archive— seeking everything that seems to apply to the current research project as it is currently understood. Two years from now, however, the scope of the research will have grown or tightened, and the same record set might need to be searched again, with new questions in mind.

I recommend that scholars with such research issues take care to document the nature of each research pass over a set of records or secondary literature. If your first pass through a set of records focused on finding information about several people you considered important to your research, make certain that your notes are clear about that specific scope of review. If you captured every reference *without exception* to people with the last name Mayberry and you searched for mentions of James (Jim and J.) Burson, record that. Otherwise you may have to go back over every mention of both to be sure your first pass was thorough.

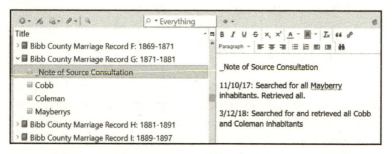

In your notes, be very specific about what you searched
for in the records under review, and the results of your search.

I recommend you create a note beneath a Zotero research record to reflect the scope of any review you have done of the material. If knowing the date you consulted the material matters, put that in your notes, as well. If this record set may change in the future—new material being added to a database, for example—the date could be valuable in knowing that you must make the same search of the records again on *new* material.

Very importantly, make a note of what you were seeking but did *not* find. It is easy to overlook this, and it is the most likely reason you will duplicate effort. Your goal in this is to prevent any need to repeat research because you are unsure of what you captured the last time. These notes can also be stored in notes attached to the research record or in a more formal log or report, if that is what your research requires.

RESEARCH-RELATED TO-DO LISTS

You will often encounter the mention of something that could be helpful to your research, if you can locate and review the resource at some point. If you have not created a structured process for handling future research needs, you will have a hard time pulling together the plan for your next research trip. You also never know when an opportunity to do research at a specific repository might spring up, with little time to plan. Now and then I find myself with an extra hour to kill, while visiting the state archives for a meeting unrelated to my research. I have a chance of using that hour well, if there is a place I have captured a to-do list for that archive.

Zotero offers the ideal research to-do list, simply by being itself. It fully integrates with research notes, reduces repetitious work, and can be accessed anywhere you have a web connection. It allows you to keep track of research questions you need to pursue, which might require work at multiple repositories. And it allows you to keep up with whether you have processed the material you have acquired—or simply gathered it. By setting up the structure below, you can do all these things.

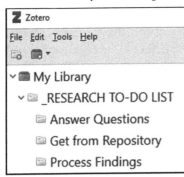

Use the Zotero Collections to create your desired to-do organization.

I have created a to-do list in Zotero by creating a collection where I drop items I need to handle, using Zotero Connector. When I want to create a priority sorting within the to-do folders, I put a number in front of the title.

I like my to-do lists to fall at the top of my Zotero library menu, so I have named my collection "_RESEARCH TO-

DO LIST," beginning with the underscore character to make it fall first in alphabetical order. Items on my research to-do list typically fall into one of these three categories:

Answer Questions keeps a working list of specific questions that require research to answer.

Get from Repository captures the reference information of items I want to review the next time I visit any of a group of repositories.

Process Findings contains items gathered in the "Get from Repository" stage, now awaiting my time to read, analyze and place my findings where they belong in my main research collections.

Now, let's look at each one more closely, with suggestions for how to manage your future research.

Answer questions

Your research will likely center on some large questions, which may never be answered simply or quickly. These major theme questions can become collections in Zotero, where you gather anything that addresses the question. But as you begin to research and write about these big questions, many small detail questions will surface—uncertainty about a date or middle initial—things that will be lost if not gathered in a tickler file. This folder allows us to keep them always in front of us, as we read and review materials.

Within the folder, I recommend that you keep a note at the top (start its title with an underscore) that describes the question or conflict that needs to be resolved. As you find new pieces of evidence that lead to the answer, you can build your explanation here for the answer you come to accept as true.

You can also drag this note into your regular research organization, wherever it is appropriate, to remind you that you have an unanswered question under review. Gather evidence in this to-do folder, until you have the answer proven to your satisfaction.

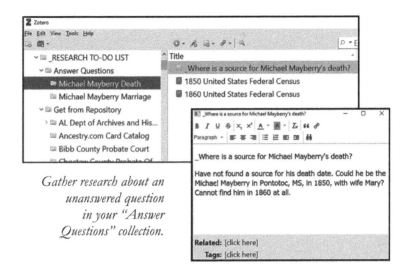

Gather research about an unanswered question in your "Answer Questions" collection.

When you have found the answer and proven it adequately, you can move the question folder from the *Answer Questions* to-do collection to its appropriate place in your research folders. In the process, you are removing it from your to-do folder, in essence, checking it off as done and documenting your answer in the process. It then becomes a place you can quickly review your logic, should it be challenged later.

For the more complex or disputed questions, I suggest that scholars use a technique I learned from the genealogy field. I have long wished I had known it when I was working on my doctoral dissertation. Genealogists use something they call a research plan to dig deeply into a factual problem.

My own GEG Research Plan design is available online at https://goldenchannelpublishing.com/shop/ if you would like to see how one is structured. You will likely create your research plan in Microsoft Word or another word processor. But store a link to it in your *Answer Questions* to-do folder. A research plan not only guides you to a solid conclusion but serves as your defense when your complicated answer is challenged by colleagues.

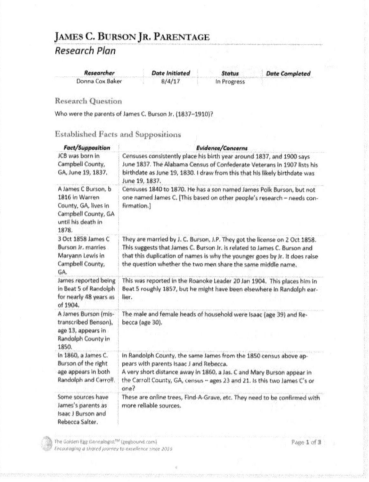

JAMES C. BURSON JR. PARENTAGE

Research Plan

Researcher	Date Initiated	Status	Date Completed
Donna Cox Baker	8/4/17	In Progress	

Research Question

Who were the parents of James C. Burson Jr. (1837–1910)?

Established Facts and Suppositions

Fact/Supposition	Evidence/Concerns
JCB was born in Campbell County, GA, June 19, 1837.	Censuses consistently place his birth year around 1837, and 1900 says June 1837. The Alabama Census of Confederate Veterans in 1907 lists his birthdate as June 19, 1830. I draw from this that his likely birthdate was June 19, 1837.
A James C Burson, b 1816 in Warren County, GA, lives in Campbell County, GA until his death in 1878.	Censuses 1840 to 1870. He has a son named James Polk Burson, but not one named James C. [This based on other people's research – needs confirmation.]
3 Oct 1858 James C Burson Jr. marries Maryann Lewis in Campbell County, GA.	They are married by J. C. Burson, J.P. They got the license on 2 Oct 1858. This suggests that James C. Burson Jr. is related to James C. Burson and that this duplication of names is why the younger goes by Jr. It does raise the question whether the two men share the same middle name.
James reported being in Beat 5 of Randolph for nearly 48 years as of 1904.	This was reported in the Roanoke Leader 20 Jan 1904. This places him in Beat 5 roughly 1857, but he might have been elsewhere in Randolph earlier.
A James Burson (mistranscribed Benson), age 13, appears in Randolph County in 1850.	The male and female heads of household were Isaac (age 39) and Rebecca (age 30).
In 1860, a James C. Burson of the right age appears in both Randolph and Carroll.	In Randolph County, the same James from the 1850 census above appears with parents Isaac and Rebecca. A very short distance away in 1860, a Jas. C and Mary Burson appear in the Carroll County, GA, census – ages 23 and 21. Is this two James C's or one?
Some sources have James's parents as Isaac J Burson and Rebecca Salter.	These are online trees, Find-A-Grave, etc. They need to be confirmed with more reliable sources.

The Golden Egg Genealogist™ (gegbound.com)
Encouraging a shared journey to excellence since 2016

Page 1 of 3

*A carefully crafted research plan can work through a
complicated question and serve as the justification that
defends the answer if later challenged.*

A great value of Zotero lies in its ability to extract bibliographic information from web pages, especially library catalogs, through the Zotero Connector (see Chapter 8). Our to-do lists are, often as not, a tickler to check out a specific resource the next time we are able to go to a certain library or archive.

Under my *Get from Repository* collection, I have a folder for any archive or collection I might need to visit or consult. I gather records here of every source that interests me. When I have the time at last to visit an archive, I have the research list ready to go. I already have my reference information entered and only need to add my findings.

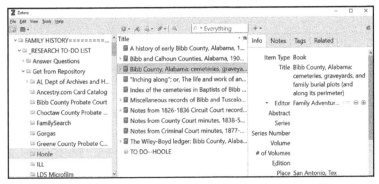

The Zotero Connector capture of bibliographic references from websites creates a quick method of identifying sources to be consulted when visiting repositories.

In this example, I have created a repository folder called "Hoole." In it, I am collecting a list of potentially useful sources from the catalog of the W. S. Stanley Hoole Special Collections Library at the University of Alabama. On the Hoole website, I see a book about Bibb County cemeteries that could answer a question about someone I am researching. Zotero Connector populates the bibliographic information in the Detail pane with one click.

I also drag the entry into a folder for Bibb County, Alabama, in my research collection, where it will remain permanently, long after it ceases to be a "to do." To this record, I will add research notes and attach PDFs of any pages I scan.

Since Zotero syncs data to its own cloud, I can get to my repository to-do list from any Internet-connected computer, including my smartphone. If I find myself able to visit a repository unexpectedly, with no time to print out to-do lists or to pack my laptop, I still know exactly what I intended to do at this archive. I can take the notes in Zotero's online environment and sync them back to my desktop software, ready for me when I get home.

Process findings

Once the research has been done in a repository, you must extract relevant details from the repository research into your research or writing project. Zotero allows you to keep a virtual in-box of data awaiting transcription, extraction, and updating.

I have two subfolders in this collection, one called *Folder in Progress* and one called *To Do Eventually*. While most of my work sits directly in *Process Findings*, these other two help me to organize priorities. *Folder in Progress* reminds me where I left off, last time I worked on extracting research notes. *To Do Eventually* is where I drop items that are of a lower priority, so I put my attention where it most needs to be.

When you do your research on paper, the photocopies and research notes you bring home from an archive can sit in a box for months and years, waiting for you to extract them. While they sit there, you cannot easily find them, if you remember you have them at all.

In Zotero, you can take all these pending items and drag them *also* into proper folders so that your filing is up to date, long before you have properly processed the data.

SUMMARY

While Zotero developers did not design it to be a to-do list or research log, it easily becomes these, with the creation of a few folders. Better, it becomes so much more than either of these could ever be in their traditional forms. It integrates all your work together in the optimal way.

Now having looked at repository research from a planning perspective, we will turn our attention to the use of Zotero on the road and online.

14: Zotero Online & on the Road

As you make decisions about how to manage knowledge for your career and its projects, you must consider the degree to which your work connects you with other people and locations. Do others need access to your work? Will you work from locations other than your desktop? Are you accessing Zotero from a tablet or smartphone?

Zotero's online environment allows you to collaborate with colleagues. You can view and update Zotero from a remote location, using a computer that does not have Zotero installed. And you can even see and update your work on your smartphone, though this feature is not quite as smooth and intuitive as it needs to be.

This chapter introduces you to these features and alerts you to special setup or operations for these online and external uses.

Collaborating and Sharing

Zotero allows you to share bibliographies or your research with others. You can share it generally, with open public accessibility, or specifically within a defined group.

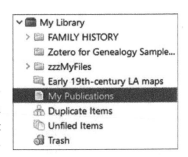

Share your research with anyone by using My Publications.

My Publications

If you are creating work you want (and have the right) to share with the public generally, you can drag the Zotero items into the *My Publications* folder in your Collections pane.

The items will form a bibliography on your profile page on Zotero.org. You may use the Abstract field to annotate them, and you can add PDFs. This offers you a way to present your

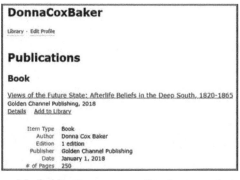

unpublished work to the public, if you desire. Zotero will place the responsibility fully and consciously on you to ensure you have the right to publish anything you upload. You will be asked to confirm it before Zotero accepts it.

My Publications creates a list of your work with open public access.

If you do not want this information to be viewed on your profile page, adjust the privacy settings on the profile. You can choose to suppress notes or to let your entire library be viewable.

Groups

Zotero offers you a facility to create groups around a specific interest or project. You were introduced to a group when you began to work on the exercises for this book. In joining the Baker's Z Solution group, material I had added to a group library showed up in your Zotero workspace. You create a group by logging into Zotero.org and choosing the Group menu option. Click **Create a New Group**. You will then set the parameters you need for your group.

If you choose to create a group that allows others to contribute, multiple people could add items, which will then appear in the *Group Libraries* section of every group member's Collections pane. Members will not be able to see what you have put into your regular, private Zotero library. You may drag and drop items between your personal and group libraries within the desktop Zotero environment. They will be copied—not moved. Unlike dragging items from one collection to another within your private library, these Zotero items will not be linked to a single source. A change to one copy will not change the other.

You control the group and its member privileges using the Group Settings option, which will appear just below the title of your group. Within the group settings, you can choose a group name (which cannot contain the word "Zotero"), create a description of the group, select academic disciplines it supports, and attach it to a URL, if you have a related website.

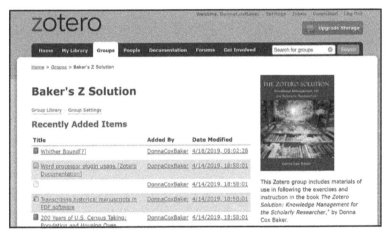

Your Zotero Group Library allows those of like interest or a shared mission to collaborate and discuss their research.

On the Group Settings view, you will also see two new settings appearing beneath the title—your Members Settings and Library Settings. In the Member Settings, your list of members appears, allowing you to set them up with either Admin or Member privileges. If you give another person "Admin" permissions, they share your power to control the group.

In the Library Settings, you determine who can find your group, who can join it, and what a member can do. Here are the setting options:

Group Type

Your group can be "Private," accessible only to those you have invited and not visible to anyone else. A group can be designated "Public, Closed," if you want it to be publicly viewable, without opening the membership, unless by invitation. A group marked "Public, Open" can be found and joined by anyone.

Library Reading

This setting determines whether the group library can be seen by the internet public or only by members.

Library Editing

This setting determines if all members can edit, add or remove items from the library, or whether it can only be done by group "admins."

File Editing

This setting determines how file attachments are handled for the group. Public, open groups cannot share files. For the other group types, you may decide whether to allow group members to handle file attachments in the shared library or whether only admins can do that. The disk space required to hold the files is counted against the account of the group owner, so you will likely want an account with unlimited space, if you choose to give group members the ability to attach files.

As the group owner, you may delete or change the group's settings at your own discretion. If you have given members the power to attach files, you should also make clear their responsibility to upload nothing for public view that is not their own, in public domain, or used with permission.

ZOTERO ON TABLETS AND SMARTPHONES

Zotero is at its best on a desktop or laptop computer, without the limits of the more limited mobile devices. But the online version of Zotero (or an iteration of it for smaller screens) can be used by tablets and smartphones.

Zotero on a smartphone

You can open Zotero.org's online library from your smartphone, and it will be reconfigured for the small screen. My Android moto z3 opens *My Library* with the collection directory and a toolbar. These instructions apply to the Android view and will likely apply to other smartphone variations.

The toolbar has a Back button on the upper left, an Edit button on the upper right, and a red Zotero dropdown list in the center to offer your Item Types. When you click **Edit**, a second row of buttons appears, allowing you to **Create**, **Edit**, or **Delete** a collection or record.

Maneuvering in your Zotero data by smartphone can be a bit awkward at first—not always predictable or consistent in its functions. You may find that it stops responding to your selections or typing. Generally refreshing the screen will correct this locking.

At the bottom of displayed records, you will also see three more buttons that can affect your functions. While working in a reference item, the Items button should be activated. While in Collections, the Collections button should be activated. Sometimes Zotero handles this for you, and sometimes it does not. But if the app seems to be behaving oddly, check these buttons to ensure the proper one is activated.

Zotero reformats its online environment to work for your smartphone.

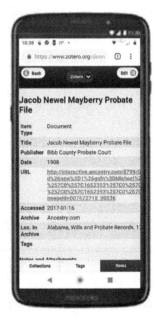

When you want to follow a URL link, you will need to double-click the link. A single click will display an error.

Zotero's usefulness for smartphones lies more in reference to viewing work already done than in adding or editing material. It is helpful, though, to know that edits can be made if needed. And new material can be added if you have the patience.

Tablets

Zotero does not yet offer a tablet application to mimic the Zotero desktop interface. At present, tablets can access your online Zotero library at Zotero.org. From there, you can view, add, and edit reference items. You can also upload attachments if they are accessible on your tablet. But you cannot create links to attachments.

Zotero is working on an iPad app, according to Dan Stillman on the Zotero forums, so we can hope that tablets' limitations will be minimized in time.* If you have both a desktop or laptop computer and a tablet, it is possible to use software like Team Viewer to remote control the computer from your tablet, which should operate Zotero as though it was installed on the tablet. Remote control does require that you leave your computer on, waiting for you to access it remotely.

ZOTERO ON THE ROAD

Zotero's ability to travel well stands as one of its most useful features. Of course, if you travel with the same laptop you use at home—the one that has Zotero installed and has all your attachments on it—a simple Wi-Fi connection at your remote site will have you working exactly as you did at home. Your entire research goes with you, and you have full power over it.

But even if you did not travel with your regular computer, you can access everything you are syncing to Zotero's cloud storage from a remote location, if you have access to a computer with an Internet connection. Any work you do in the

---

* See https://forums.zotero.org/discussion/comment/333622#Comment_333622.

online version will sync back to your home computer, when you return home.

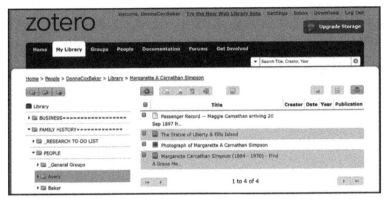

Zotero.org allows you to access all of the material you have synced from your desktop data.

The online version of Zotero operates very similarly to the desktop version, and special instructions should not be needed. Let your cursor sit above a button on its toolbar, and you will be told what it does.

As we discussed in Chapter 5, while working on your computer with Zotero installed, you have the choice of embedding your attachments into Zotero or linking to them externally. If you chose to embed them, the attachments will be available to you when you log in to the online version of Zotero on a remote computer. The ability to read the attachments, of course, depends on whether the remote computer you are using has the appropriate software for the specific attachment (Word, Excel, etc.).

If you linked to attachments outside of Zotero, you will not be able to open them from within the online Zotero interface on someone else's computer. However, if you are storing your attachments in a cloud environment, you will be able to find and open them from your cloud service (again, assuming you have the appropriate software on the computer you are using remotely).

Using Zotero's online environment and the cloud for attachments, you can have all of your research notes with you, with no effort. Even if you did not have time to plan your research trip, it is there.

Summary

As the body of knowledge you capture grows throughout your career, the value of remote access to it expands. If the work has all been done in Zotero, your research is always at your fingertips. No file cabinets or boxes being lugged from place to place. Not even a binder.

Before we wrap up this overview of Zotero, we will turn to a few last tips and tricks to maximize the experience.

15: MORE ZOTERO TOPICS

As we approach the end of this book, I do not pretend to have covered all that can be known about Zotero. Developers continue to improve and expand its value, and I continue to discover more features and new uses for Zotero all the time. An entire book could be written, no doubt, exclusively on methods to create and edit Zotero styles. But before we depart, there are a few more things I want to show you.

EDIT IN A SEPARATE WINDOW

When you get ready to take notes in Zotero, you often need to display something else on the screen at the same time. Zotero allows you to detach a note into a separate and sizable window, for placement wherever it is convenient for your notetaking. I mentioned this feature in Chapter 3, but I wanted to give it a bit more attention.

In a Zotero note, when you click the **Edit in a separate window** button, Zotero extracts your notes to a free-standing window with your editing tools. You can resize the window and move it anywhere on the screen you find useful. It will also allow you to open multiple windows at the same time.

This is particularly helpful if you are taking notes from a website or other application also displayed on your screen. It allows you to move the bulk of Zotero out of sight while you continue to take notes. You can make the notes window narrow and tall, short and wide, or a small square in a corner.

This feature is also useful if you are consulting your notes while working in other software. Let's say you are writing an article or book, based on your research. This allows you to have your word-processing software open over much of your screen, with your research displayed in as tight a space as you need.

Transcribing manuscripts

Those in fields like history, genealogy, religious studies, anthropology, linguistics, and many other fields are required to transcribe old handwritten documents. You can transcribe from a scan of the original directly into Zotero notes in the freestanding window. This creates a fully searchable document where there was

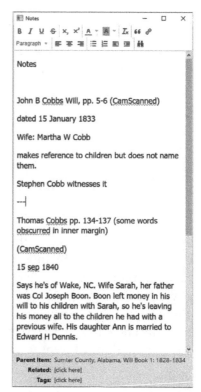

Zotero allows you to open your notes in sizable, movable windows, moving them into available space around other tools.

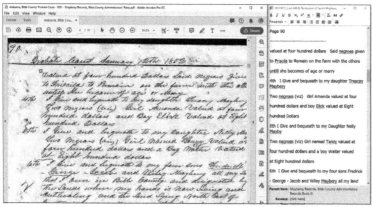

Zotero becomes your manuscript transcription tool when you choose to edit your note in a separate window.

once just a graphic of handwriting. Both the manuscript scan and the transcription can be attachments to the Zotero citation.

ZOTEROBIB

The development team that brought us Zotero has created an online tool called ZoteroBib to enable the quick production of a bibliography. The tool requires no software installation and it works from virtually any device with a web browser. The tool is available at:

https://zbib.org/

This product is ideal for a one-time task. If your research will be used for multiple purposes, the full Zotero product make more sense.

It makes use of some of the same tools—the ability to extract reference information using the source's title or a URL, ISBN, DOI, PMIS, or arXiv ID. It can pull information as Zotero Connector does, also. And it offers manual entry of citation data.

ZoteroBib can be used while you are writing a paper. You can pull the footnote or endnote citation from your bibliographic reference and paste it into your paper. Then you can paste the full bibliography, fully formed at the end. It offers formatting in these styles: *American Psychological Association 6th edition, Chicago Manual of Style 17th edition, Modern Language Association 8th edition,* and *Turabian 8th edition.*

This tool saves your bibliography out to your browser's local storage while you are working. You can also create a link to the bibliography if you want to access it later.

RETRACTION WATCH

Zotero has begun the integration of its data with Retraction Watch, a database of the Center for Scientific Integrity. The center identifies published research that has been retracted by its publisher, if it has been deemed unworthy for any reason. Zotero's warnings about retracted articles are set up to alert you not only when you add such a record to your database, but also after the fact. If you have already used a retracted article in your work, several layers of warning ensure that you know that your own work might have been affected by the withdrawal of this research from the academy.

Currently, Zotero can only match Retraction Watch records that share a DOI or PMID with the record you have entered. Developers are working on broader matching criteria, which should be included in a future release.

If a record you have in your Zotero database is flagged by Retraction Watch, based on its DOI or PMID, Zotero will notify you in several ways. First, you will be notified by a warning message at the top of your Research List, on a red bar, saying:

An item in your database has been retracted. <u>View item</u>.

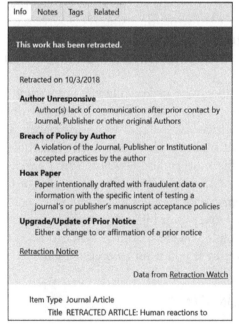

Zotero will insert a list of the violations that resulted in the retraction of the article and a link to the full notice online.

You can view the record by clicking the <u>View item</u> link. Above the Zotero record, it will insert a detailed description of the reasons the item was retracted and a link to the Retraction Notice on Retraction Watch. This warning will only show temporarily, but two other layers of warning will remain in place.

Title	Creator	Date Added
⌄ ☐ ✗ RETRACTED ARTICLE: Human reactions to...	Wilson	7/10/2019, 9:53:48 PM

The Research List flags all retracted articles by inserting text in the Title field.

Zotero will insert "*RETRACTED ARTICLE:" in front of the title name in your Research List. You will also see that a new item called "Retracted Items" in your Collections pane, which will show you a list of all things that have been flagged as retracted. This will ensure that you cannot use the source again without being aware of the potential problem.

It is important, however, to be aware that some people have detected false flags on sources. So always seek confirmation before eliminating the source entirely from consideration in your research or making any sort of public announcement that it has been retracted.

RSS FEEDS

Zotero allows you to set up RSS (Really Simple Syndication) feeds to aggregate posts from an external website. Create a new RSS Feed by selecting the **New Library** button on the Zotero toolbar, then RSS Feed and your feed method of choose—usually URL.

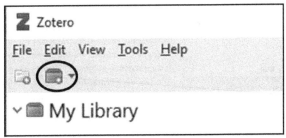

The icon to the right of the New Collection button offers a New Feed option.

The RSS Feed by URL setup is quite simple. You enter the URL your feed requires, give it your desired label, and decide how often you want to get an update and how long you want to keep the stories. For the OPML option, you browse for the proper file on your hard drive.

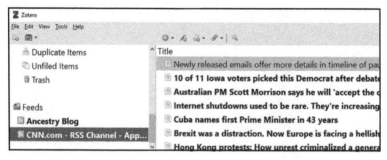

Enter your RSS Feed's URL and any other
desired parameters.

New material from your chosen RSS Feed sources are automatically presented when you are in Zotero. The source is displayed below your Trash bin in the Collections pane. The story titles appear in the Research List and are cited as Journal Articles in the Details pane. You can follow the URL to read the article online, or you can choose **Add to Library** at the top of the pane and make it a standard research item.

Feeds are available from the bottom of your Collections pane.

SUMMARY

Your discovery of the many wonders of Zotero will come with exploration. When you find yourself wondering if it will do something I have not covered, ask. The online forum at Zotero is rich with secrets and has a remarkable responsiveness. Many of the features I have described to you came to my attention when I asked a question on the forum.

Now, give me just a moment more and read the very brief conclusion for clues about where to go from here.

16: CONCLUSION

I hope this book has encouraged you to try Zotero. As your research and notetaking tool, it offers so much more than many tools I have tried. Even as I prepared to write this book, I kept discovering new features.

Our expanding support of the Corporation for Digital Scholarship will enable further development of the technology. Please consider supporting this vital organization by donating, opting for the paid storage option, and/or by telling colleagues and students about Zotero.

Join our Facebook site for continuing tips, encouragement, solutions, and ideas. You can find us by searching Facebook for this book title:

The Zotero Solution: Knowledge Management for the Scholarly Researcher

We will not attempt to supersede the outstanding support you will find at https://forums.zotero.org/discussions. Experienced users are very quick to answer questions and guide the rest of us. I encourage you to pose any technical support questions there first. If you are not getting the answers you need there, we would be happy to have you broach the subject on our Facebook page, in case we can get creative with solutions.

I trust you will find Zotero to be the excellent support for scholarly research that I have. It has been my tool of choice for nearly a decade now. That it happens to be free, I consider a nice bonus. Enjoy your Zotero journey!

Index

ABOUT THE AUTHOR

Donna Cox Baker began her writing and editing career in technical communications for a Fortune 500 computer corporation. Discovering a passion for genealogy and history, she made a move into historical publishing in 2002 and eventually earned a PhD in history. Since 2002, she has directed the *Alabama Heritage* magazine team at the University of Alabama, and she acquired history manuscripts for the University of Alabama Press for seven years.

She authored *Views of the Future State: Afterlife Beliefs in the Deep South, 1820–1865* (2018) and *Zotero for Genealogy: Harnessing the Power of Your Research* (2019)—both from Golden Channel

Publishing. Also in 2019, she coedited new scholarship by a team of Alabama historians in *Alabama from Territory to Statehood: An Alabama Heritage Bicentennial Collection* (NewSouth Books). She has published numerous articles on history and genealogy.

Baker manages her own blog about family history at the *Golden Egg Genealogist* (gegbound.com). She also cofounded the *Beyond Kin Project* (beyondkin.org), which encourages the descendants of slaveholders to take up the mission of documenting the family history of the whole plantation—black and white. Her early days in the computer industry created in her a desire to find better, faster, and more efficient ways to get things done. She is particularly interested in eliminating wasted time and effort in genealogical and historical research. She considers Zotero a critical part of that mission.

MORE FROM GOLDEN CHANNEL PUBLISHING

Early Federal Census Worksheet

Take the pain out of attempting to extract meaning from the early federal censuses from 1790 to 1860. Enjoy either the Premium Edition for Microsoft Excel's desktop software or the Lite edition for Excel Online. Download both simple-to-use versions for a single low price. Put hundreds of census entries in a single sheet or make as many copies as you need for your own personal use, at no additional cost.

GEG Research Plan

Truly reliable genealogical research requires a committed focus on getting the right answer—not the expedient one. And should our conclusion ever be challenged, we need to demonstrate how we came to it. A research plan creates that focus, defining the question, creating a plan to answer it, and documenting the path to the conclusion. A blank GEG Research Plan can be saved as a document template in Microsoft Word or simply copied as a new document for each research question you pursue. Combining elegant form and thorough function, this research plan looks as good as it works.

goldenchannelpublishing.com

The Golden Egg Genealogist
Manifesting the treasures of ancestry. A shared journey.

gegbound.com

The Beyond Kin Project
For every soul a story, a family, a name.

beyondkin.org

goldenchannelpublishing.com

Zotero for Genealogy
Harnessing the Power of Your Research

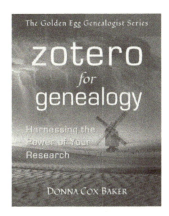

by
Donna Cox Baker

2019 159 pp.
142 B&W figures
97809996899-1-2

Zotero offers genealogists a powerful and versatile citation manager, an endless file cabinet, go-anywhere access to research, a flexible organizational structure, and the ability to file one thing in many places. Developed originally by George Mason University and used by scholars worldwide, this robust product serves research in phenomenal ways. Best of all, for all its value, Zotero is free to download.

An avid Zotero user since graduate school, author Donna Cox Baker proves it to be the perfect complement to genealogical research. Not only does it eliminate file cabinets, binders, and stacks of unfiled papers, it brings your voluminous research anywhere you have Internet access. *Zotero for Genealogy* teaches Zotero from installation to advance add-ons, using exercises and illustrations to enhance the learning experience. Baker teaches readers how to get the most out of Zotero and shares the various methods she has developed to maximize its value to genealogy.

goldenchannelpublishing.com

Views of the Future State
Afterlife Beliefs in the Deep South, 1820–1865

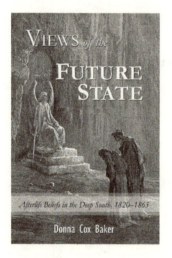

by
Donna Cox Baker

2018 250 pp.
8 B&W figures
978-0-9996899-0-5

Views of the Future State examines shifting conceptions of the afterlife among literate inhabitants of the antebellum and Civil War–era Deep South. The relatively static 1820 views of a dualistic heaven and hell took on a vibrant complexity by 1865. The challenges of scientific discoveries, universalism, mesmerism, spiritualism, Swedenborgianism, and finally war encouraged bold questioning. Southerners no longer focused primarily on how to get to heaven, as they had done for generations. The seekers among them thirsted for detailed depictions of the celestial realms. They were particularly intrigued with those who claimed to have first-hand experience of heaven.

Afterlife beliefs then, as now, encompassed a complex and dynamic spectrum of thought. Baker begins to offer shape to the spectrum by examining the outer fringes of acceptable questioning—the place where orthodox religious people actively resisted deviations in thought and method by the seekers and skeptics in their midst.

Analyzing the voluminous writings of this era and the evidence of public consumption of and debate over them, Baker takes readers on a fascinating human journey. *Views of the Future State* presents a much-needed chapter in the heritage of spiritual seekers and raises timeless questions about life after death.

goldenchannelpublishing.com